SMALL ARMS AND THE SECURITY DEBATE IN SOUTH ASIA

The Regional Centre for Strategic Studies (RCSS) is an independent, non-profit and non-governmental organization for collaborative research, networking and interaction on strategic and international issues pertaining to South Asia. Set up in 1992, the RCSS is based in Colombo, Sri Lanka.

The RCSS is a South Asian forum for studies, training and multi-track dialogue and deliberation on issues of regional interest. All activities of RCSS are designed with a South Asia focus and are usually participated by experts from all South Asian countries. The Centre is envisaged as a forum for advancing the cause of co-operation, security, conflict resolution, confidence building, peace and development in the countries of the South Asian region.

The RCSS serves its South Asian and international constituency by: (a) networking programmes that promote interaction, communication and exchange between institutions and individuals within and outside the region engaged in South Asian strategic studies; (b) organizing regional workshops and seminars and sponsoring and coordinating collaborative research; and (c) disseminating output of the research through publications which include books, monographs and a quarterly newsletter. The RCSS facilitates scholars and other professionals of South Asia to address, mutually and collectively, problems and issues of topical interest for all countries of the region.

Queries may be addressed to:

Regional Centre for Strategic Studies
2 Elibank Road
Colombo 5
SRI LANKA
Tel: (94-11) 2599734, 599735
Fax: 2599993; e-mail: rcss@sri.lanka.net
RCSS website: http://www.rcss.org

RCSS Policy Studies 33

Small Arms and the Security Debate in South Asia

SALMA MALIK
MALLIKA JOSEPH

REGIONAL CENTRE FOR STRATEGIC STUDIES
COLOMBO

MANOHAR
2005

Published by
Ajay Kumar Jain for
Manohar Publishers & Distributors
4753/23 Ansari Road, Daryaganj
New Delhi 110 002
and
Regional Centre for Strategic Studies
2 Elibank Road
Colombo 5
SRI LANKA
Tel: (94-11) 2599734-5; Fax: 2599993;
e-mail: rcss@sri.lanka.net
Website: http://www.rcss.org

First published 2005

ISBN 81-7304-625-5

Typeset by
Kohli Print
Delhi 110 051

Printed at
Lordson Publishers Pvt. Ltd.
Delhi 110 007

Distributed in South Asia by
FOUNDATION BOOKS
4381/4, Ansari Rorad
Daryaganj, New Delhi 110 002
and its branches at Mumbai, Hyderabad,
Bangalore, Chennai, Kolkata

Contents

RCSS is grateful to the
Ford Foundation for its generous
support for the Mahbub-ul-Haq Award
on which this report is based.

The proliferation of small arms, and munitions and explosives has also aggravated the violence associated with terrorism and organized crime. Even in societies not beset by civil war, the easy availability of small arms has in many cases contributed to violence and political instability. These, in turn, have damaged development prospects and imperiled human security in every way.

Kofi Annan, UN Secretary General

Preface

The presence of small arms and light weapons is inimical to State as well as human security. Banning their use, like that of landmines, is a Utopian concept best left to some sections of the civil society engaged in advocacy. We take particular care to mention 'some sections', because even the civil society rightly finds the issue of banning small arms too Utopian and problematic to handle. There is concurrence, however, that with appropriate measures the flow and use of weapons can be restricted to a large extent. And even if only some portions of it can be accomplished, a great service to humanity would have been achieved.

Actually, anything that can be said on small arms has already been said. This holds true for South Asia as well. What can be done is only a periodical updating of statistics. So the challenge was how to introduce the small arms debate in the security discourse of South Asia without appearing insipid and repetitive. And this at a time when there is an oscillation between two thresholds of the security discourse—State security, and human security.

What we have attempted in this monograph is to introduce the subject in the overlapping areas of the two spheres of security thought. This was possible because the proliferation of small arms affects the State as well as the society. Viewed either through prisms of State or of human security, small arms constitute a grave threat.

Issues pertaining to the increased use of explosives and illegal domestic production have also been introduced, which have not received the attention they merit. We have made a modest attempt to highlight the need for including explosive devices and illegal domestic production in any discourse on small arms.

The study has its limitations, as we have been unable to equally represent the situations prevailing in South Asian countries other than India and Pakistan. We have made a humble attempt to build a case for a looking at the issue of small arms and light weapons in a more serious and comprehensive manner than is currently being done.

A case exists for regional cooperation among the South Asian countries. There are best practices within the region, which can be emulated, but only to an extent. The situations prevailing in each country are unique and call for targeted solutions. However, a space exists for regional cooperation to arrest the further inflow of arms in the region from neighbouring conflict zones. This space needs to be explored. We hope this monograph will help in exploiting that space by highlighting the vulnerable situation the South Asian countries are placed in.

September 2004

SALMA MALIK
MALLIKA JOSEPH

Introduction

Beset by varying degrees of violent conflict resulting from nation building, religious fundamentalism, insurgency, separatism, terrorism, left extremism, and caste politics, security in South Asia is further exacerbated by gunrunning, drug trafficking, money laundering, and organized crime conglomerates that sustain and fuel some of these conflicts. The dialectics of these violent conflicts not only endanger the sovereignty of the State by slow erosion of its authority, but, most importantly, they also create a sense of vulnerability among its citizens by impinging on all aspects of human security. While misgovernance, corruption and State violence do exacerbate the situation, the easy availability of small arms and their unscrupulous use can easily be identified as the most important element that triggers and sustains human insecurity.

The end of the Cold War brought forth a dialectic change in the traditional debate on security and ushered in discourses on a whole range of non-military challenges to security, including small arms. Unfortunately, this change is not yet reflected in the region, where emphasis is primarily on enhancing military postures and capabilities, and persistent tensions between India and Pakistan backed by their nuclear prowess have stifled non-military security concerns not only in their countries, but also in the region as a whole.

The Programme of Action (POA) adopted at the 2001 United Nations Conference on the Illicit Trade in Small Arms and Light Weapons in All Its Aspects is the first international effort by states to look at the issue of small arms proliferation within the ambit of State security. However, as the title suggests, the focus is only on illicit trade, and falls short of comprehensively addressing issues relating to illegal domestic production.

Within the region, cooperation on this issue is abysmal, with countries blaming each other as the sources of weapons. Plugging supply from outside the region through cooperative regional measures would definitely contribute to reducing the scale of violence in the various theatres of conflict. However, cooperation *within* the region could also achieve positive results. Instances when Bangladesh security forces seized weapons from insurgents from India's north-east operating from Bangladesh, or when Indian security forces seized weapons bound for Maoists in Nepal, indicate that meaningful cooperation is possible.

With inadequate global measures and non-synchronized regional efforts unable to address the proliferation and use of small arms adequately, states have indulged in limited national measures that have brought about mixed results. For example, in autumn 2000, the Pakistan government initiated a national Arms Control Campaign to facilitate de-weaponization through the confiscation and prosecution of illegally held arms. Initially, owners were encouraged to register licenced weapons. During the second stage, owners could surrender illegal firearms over a two-week amnesty in June 2001. This arms recovery and de-weaponization campaign was unique in the sense that compared to earlier arms-recovery efforts worldwide, this campaign was government initiated and very well organized. Bangladesh has been involved in a similar de-weaponization exercise under the guise of an anti-terrorism drive, which again has brought mixed results.

The aim of this study is to refocus non-traditional security challenges, particularly those arising from the proliferation of small arms, into the predominantly realist security debate in the region.

Chapter 1 attempts to locate the small arms discourse within the parameters of State and human security. Chapter 2 deals specifically with the scale of arms proliferation in the region, particularly from angles of supply (global illegal stockpiles, illicit trafficking and illegal production) and demand (militants, insurgents, Nepal Maoists, caste armies, fundamental groups, tribal groups, organized crime syndicates, individuals). Chapter 3 discusses efforts taken globally to address the scourge of small arms.

In particular, the chapter details the strides taken by the UN POA. Chapter 4 explores the thus far neglected realm of the problem of small arms—illegal domestic production, and Improvised Explosive Devices (IED). Chapter 5 attempts to locate some of the measures adopted by individual states to stem the proliferation of weapons. The concluding chapter is a list of suggestions/recommendations and best practices that can be adopted at national, regional and international levels to comprehensively address the problems emanating from small arms and light weapons.

Abbreviations

APLM	Anti-Personnel Land Mines
Art.	Article
AT	Anti-Tank
BLT	Bodo Liberation Tigers
BASIC	British American Security Information Council
CHRI	Commonwealth Human Rights Initiative
CIA	Central Intelligence Agency (of the USA)
DAK	Darra Adam Khel
DHD	Dima Halong Daoga
EU	European Union
GIIS	Graduate Institute of International Studies
G-8	Group of Eight States
Harkat	Harkat-ul-Ansar
HDI	Human Development Index
HGI	Humane Governance Index
IED	Improvised Explosive Devices
IANSA	International Action Network on Small Arms
ICRC	International Committee of the Red Cross
IPCS	Institute of Peace and Conflict Studies
ISI	Inter-Services Intelligence
J&K	Jammu and Kashmir
LAWs	Light Anti-Tank Weapons
LeT	Lashkar-e-Toiba
LMG	Light Machine Gun
LTTE	Liberation Tigers of Tamil Eelam
LW	Light Weapons
MBRL	Multi-Barrel Rocket Launcher
MCC	Maoist Communist Centre

MULTA	Muslim United Liberation Tigers of Asom (or Assam)
NDFB	National Democratic Front of Bodoland
NGO	Non-Governmental Organization
9/11	11 September 2001
NISAT	Norwegian Initiative on Small Arms Transfers
NNC	Naga National Council
NOC	No Objection Certificate
NSA	Non-State Actor
NSCN	National Socialist Council of Nagaland
NWFP	North-West Frontier Province
OAS	Organization of American States
PDS	Public Distribution System
POA	Programme of Action to Prevent, Combat and Eradicate the Illicit Trade in Small Arms and Light Weapons in All Its Aspects
POF	Pakistan Ordinance Factories
PWG	People's War Group
RAW	Research & Analysis Wing (of Indian Intelligence)
RCSS	Regional Centre for Strategic Studies
RDX	Research Developed Explosive (common name for cyclotrimethylene tri-nitramine, a powerful explosive)
RPG	Rocket Propelled Grenade
SA	Small Arms
SA/LW or SALW	Small Arms and Light Weapons
SAARC	South Asian Association for Regional Cooperation
SAP	South Asia Partnership International (a Sri Lanka-based organization)
SAM	Surface-to-Air Missile
SRO	Statutory Regulatory Orders

UN Small Arms Conference	UN Conference on the Illicit Trade in Small Arms and Light Weapons in All Its Aspects
UAV	Unmanned Aerial Vehicle
ULFA	United Liberation Front of Asom (or Assam)
UNDP	United Nations Development Programme
UNHCR	UN High Commissioner for Refugees
UNIDIR	UN Institute for Disarmament Research
UNPOA	United Nations Programme of Action
UPDS	United Peoples Democratic Solidarity
UP	Uttar Pradesh

CHAPTER 1

Small Arms: Endangering State and Human Security

For most of the twentieth century, the practice of warfare typically entailed a series of armed encounters between the organized military forces of established states, usually for the purpose of territorial conquest or other clearly defined objectives. But the conflicts of the current era bear little resemblance to this model, as most take place within the borders of a single state. Furthermore, they entail attacks by irregular forces on unarmed civilians for the purpose of pillage, intimidation, and/or ethnic slaughter.

SMALL ARMS AND STATE SECURITY

During a period of 10 years, from 1989 to 1999, there have been 110 armed conflicts in 73 locations around the world. Categorizing these conflicts, an interesting fact emerges that 94 of these conflicts were intrastate, 9 intrastate with foreign intervention, and 7 interstate. In 1999, there were 37 active conflicts in 28 locations out of which, with the exception of two, i.e. India–Pakistan and Eritrea–Ethiopia, all were intrastate.[1] And most of these were fought with weapons that come under the somewhat misleading category of 'Small Arms and Light Weapons'.

Defining Small Arms and Light Weapons

In 1997, the United Nations General Assembly approved and refined definitions for the following categories of small arms and light weapons:

[1] Margareta Solenberg, ed., 'States in Armed Conflict 1993', Report No. 55, Uppsala: Department of Peace and Conflict Research, Uppsala University, 1994.

- *Small Arms*: Revolvers and self-loading pistols, rifles and carbines, sub-machine guns, assault rifles and light machine guns.
- *Light Weapons*: Heavy machine guns, hand-held under-barrel and mounted grenade launchers, portable anti-aircraft guns and recoilless rifles, portable launchers of anti-tank missiles and rocket systems, portable launchers of anti-aircraft missile systems and mortars of calibre less than 100 mm.
- *Ammunition and Explosives*: Cartridges (rounds) for small arms, shells and missiles for light weapons, anti-personnel and anti-tank grenades, landmines, mobile containers with missiles or shells for single action and anti-aircraft and anti-tank systems and finally explosives.[2]

Estimates of the number of small arms and light weapons in circulation range from approximately 550 million, with 50–80 million being AK-47 assault rifles.[3] An increasing number of countries are becoming self-sufficient in the manufacture of small arms and related ammunition either through indigenous or through licenced production. It has been reported that an AK-47 assault rifle can be purchased on the streets of some countries for as little as $10 (US), or in developing countries in exchange for a chicken or a goat. In other countries, criminals can rent AK-47s by the hour solely for the purpose of carrying out a criminal act. International transfers are also a major source of small arms and light weapons supply through a host of channels, both legal and illegal.[4]

South Asia has been unfortunate in inheriting similar patterns of violent conflict where most of these wars are fought with small

[2] Statement of Secretary General Kofi Annan for the 1997 UN Report of the Panel of Governmental Experts on Small Arms and Light Weapons, United Nations document A/52/298, August 1997.

[3] Graduate Institute for International Studies (GIIS), 'Half a Billion and Still Counting . . . Global Firearms Stockpiles', *The Small Arms Survey: Profiling the Problem*, Oxford: Oxford University Press, 2001, Chap. 2, p. 59.

[4] Herbert L. Calhoun, 'Small Arms and Light Weapons: Can they be Controlled?' in the United States Department of State, *Small Arms and Light Weapons: US Policy and Views, US Foreign Policy Agenda*, electronic journal of the US Department of State, vol. 6, no. 2, June 2001, p. 34.

arms which include pistols, automatic rifles, sub-machine guns, mortars, grenades, shoulder/vehicle-mounted light missiles, and landmines. With continuing violent conflicts in Kashmir, India's north-east, Sri Lanka, and Nepal, apart from the continued domestic unrest and violence spawned by religious and ethnic intolerance, South Asia is a hotbed of violent conflicts and a region where illegal weapons exist in plenty. Sandwiched between two conflict hot zones awash with weapons and narcotics (Afghanistan and Cambodia), South Asia is plagued by a situation where easy availability of illegal weapons has made the resolution of long-standing disputes virtually impossible: interstate tensions have only exacerbated the situation.

The conflict is directly related to the fact that there are some three million weapons out of the control of state machinery, with more coming in primarily from Afghanistan and South-East Asia.[5] Pakistan has been the hardest hit with the largest concentration of weapons, the source being the CIA-sponsored arms pipeline to the Afghan militia through Pakistan in the 1980s. The fallout is that the frontier region of Pakistan, or the Darra Bara, has become the Main Open Arms Bazaar. A number of underground arms bazaars are evident—Cox Bazaar (Bangladesh), and in areas outside major urban centres such as Mumbai and Delhi, and an expanding pipeline coming in via Nepal and Myanmar.

Simply put, the availability of small arms and light weapons has militarized societal discontent and empowered a variety of Non-State Actors (NSA) of all kinds. Facing them, the police and paramilitary forces often let loose a reign of terror under pressure to regain control the situation.

As the dialectics of warfare changed, so did the nature of the casualties; over 80 per cent of the casualties are now civilians. Almost 90 per cent of these casualties are caused by small arms. However, the use of small arms in these conflicts does not in any way reduce the costs, scope or destruction. The present condition

[5] This includes 35,000 in India, 100,000 in Karachi, at least a million along the frontier, a gun per family in Baluchistan, and at least 10,000–12,000 with the Tamil Tigers.

of Afghanistan is the direct result of more than US $6 billion worth of weapon's aid (mostly in the form of small weapons) sent into the country by a superpower and sympathetic allies through a conduit third country.

The direct impact of small arms on civilians is tremendous. Firearms kill more than 500,000 people each year including 200,000 in the so-called peaceful countries; millions more are injured.[6] By one estimate, approximately 2 million children have been killed as a result of armed conflict since 1990.[7]

Apart from the direct effects of small arms, the rippling effects these weapons have had on society, albeit indirect, are unfathomable. The war in Afghanistan alone is responsible for a refugee population of around 4.5 million. At the end of 1997, there were more than 22 million refugees and displaced people the world over who had had to flee their homes under hostile circumstances.[8]

The negative effects of the proliferation and illicit trafficking of small arms and light weapons have been far-reaching and diverse. Although most important are the increased threats to international and regional security, other negative aspects of these weapons include their increased use by terrorists, heightened threats to humanitarian relief workers, undermining of the implementation of peace agreements, and as impediments to fundamental development work.

While small arms and light weapons play a significant role in worsening conflicts that exact enormous human and socio-economic

[6] Robert Muggah, 'Perceptions of Small Arms Availability and Use Among Oxfam-GB Field Personnel', *Small Arms Survey*, a joint collaborative study of Oxfam and Small Arms Survey, 2000, p. 10. Also see David Anere, and Basil Massey, 'The Impact of the Use of Small Arms and Light Weapons in Conflicts: The Need for a UN Convention and Control', unpublished, Uppsala: Department of Peace and Conflict Research, Uppsala University, 30 May 2001.

[7] Graca Machel, 'Report on the Impact of Armed Conflict on Children', December 2000: http://193.135.156.14/webpub/dcihome/253e.html.

[8] Inge Kaul, Isabelle Grunberg, and Marc A. Stern, eds., *Global Public Goods: International Cooperation in the 21st Century*, 1999, p. 394. This figure is based on estimates provided by the Statistical Unit of the United Nations High Commissioner for Refugees.

costs, the causes of such conflicts lie in political, economic, ethnic and religious differences and disparities. These are often aggravated by governance-related deficiencies, such as exclusionary and repressive policies, and lack of—or weaknesses in—democratic institutions, respect for the rule of law, and human rights observance. However, the easy availability of small arms and light weapons effectively stifles government measures for addressing some of these crucial issues relating to human development and security. The government's inability to meet the just aspirations of its people *vis-à-vis* providing even some of their basic needs, further increases discontent and discord.

Owing to the large-scale and protracted nature of damage caused by small arms, development has suffered greatly. A World Bank reports notes: 'Conflict can destroy human capital gains and development investment that took decades to accumulate.'[9] The crux of the problem is global availability of light weapons out of state control, which has fuelled conflict worldwide, and prevented peacekeeping and conflict management from making perceptible dents in any of these areas.

HUMAN SECURITY

The changing dynamics of conflict have highlighted the need for a more elastic concept of security that can accommodate the newer threats to security emerging from a whole range of non-traditional security. Clearly, there is no denying that the proliferation of illegal weapons undermines State authority directly, apart from triggering the forced displacement of populations, damaging developmental infrastructure, and destroying local economies. A clear threat to the State as an institution exists. But how to reconcile the traditional notion of security discourse, tied to territorial challenge, with a larger and more comprehensive discourse that encompasses 'soft' security issues like small arms, environment, energy, and health?

[9] United Nations Development Programme (UNDP), *Human Development Report 1994*, New York: Oxford University Press, 1994.

The result has been the predominance of the idea of human security. Although presented as a global template on which to fundamentally recast the security philosophies and policies of countries to reflect the changing conditions and principles of the world order, human security has also been an instrument of national strategic priorities which often have strong domestic roots. So far, the concept of human security has been multidimensionally presented as a means of reducing the human costs of violent conflict, or as a strategy to enable governments to address basic human needs and offset the inequities of globalization. Similarly, it is also defined as a framework for providing social safety nets to people impoverished and marginalized by sudden and severe economic crises.[10]

Human security is a distinctive notion, which goes well beyond all earlier attempts to 'redefine' and broaden the realist paradigm of 'national security'. The areas of issue that encompass security are now determined by people's needs, and that automatically brings in not only military security, but also other realms crucial to people's security—economic life, environment, politics, and so on.

The idea of human security is generally thought to go back to the United Nations Development Programme report of 1994. Closely associated with the idea from the beginning was the consulting economist, the late Dr Mahbub-ul Haq, who had earlier played a key role in the construction of the Human Development Index (HDI), and who was subsequently the moving force behind the more recent Humane Governance Index (HGI). Haq's approach is outlined in his *New Imperatives of Human Security* (RGICS Paper No. 17, Rajiv Gandhi Institute for Contemparary Studies [RGICS], Rajiv Gandhi Foundation, New Delhi, 1994).

Haq answers the question of 'security for whom' quite simply. Human security is not about States and nations, but about indi-

[10] Amitav Acharya, 'Debating Human Security: East Versus the West', at the GIIS, proceedings of the Conference on Human Security and Human Development Linkages organized by the Programme for Strategic and International Studies, Geneva, 8–9 March 2001.

viduals and people. Thus, he argues that the world is 'entering a new era of human security' in which 'the entire concept of security will change—and change dramatically'. In this new conception, security will be equated with the 'security of individuals, not just security of their nations', or, to put it differently, 'security of people, not just security of territory'. Elsewhere, more normatively, he writes, 'We need to fashion a new concept of human security that is reflected in the lives of our people, not in the weapons of our country.'

TABLE 1.1: NATIONAL SECURITY AND HUMAN SECURITY

	National Security	Human Security
Security for whom	Primarily, the State.	Primarily, the individual.
Security of what values	Territorial integrity and national independence.	Personal safety and individual freedom.
Security from what threats	Direct threats from other states.	Direct threats from states and NSAs, plus indirect threats.
Security by what means	• Force as the primary instrument of security, to be used unilaterally for a state's own safety. • Balance of power is important; power is equated with military capabilities. • Cooperation between states is tenuous beyond alliance relations. • Norms and institutions are of limited value, particularly in the security/military sphere.	• Force as a secondary instrument, to be used primarily for cosmopolitan ends and collectively; sanctions, human development, and humane goverance is key instruments of individual-centred security. • Balance of power is of limitd utility; soft power is increasingly important. • Cooperation between states, international organizations and NGOs can be effective and sustained. • Norms and institutions matter; democratization and representativeness in institutions enhance their effectiveness.

Source: Kanti Bajpai, *Human Security: Concept and Measurement*, Joan B. Kroc Institute for International Peace Studies, August 2000.

SMALL ARMS AND HUMAN SECURITY

Where do small arms figure in the predominant debate on human security? Small arms are a prime ingredient of the new wars. Cast as tribal, religious or ethnic conflicts, a growing number of 'communal' conflicts are actually resource-based clashes: long-term conflicts motivated by profit, or violence generated by scarcity and inequality. Indeed, it is now clear that light weapons are more likely to be used in societies of low to medium human development, weak governance, and falling per capita income. Small arms themselves are frequently assuming the status of a currency. Guns from enduring conflicts are often hidden or stowed away by a variety of actors for later use, traded in informal markets and across frontiers, or trafficked via international brokers and criminal syndicates at exceptional returns. Criminal and informal economies throughout Africa, Central America and Eastern Europe often profit from the recirculation and reuse of small arms—undermining what are often frugal development gains.

Real and perceived insecurities of civilians fuel increased proliferation and use of arms. Arms availability in such regions is swelling and exacting a high price both in terms of lives lost and in development costs. As a result, small arms and light weapons, including military-style weapons designed for trained and organized militaries, are now in civilian hands and increasingly used in contravention of international humanitarian law and human rights. These arms, circulating from conflict to conflict (or criminal syndicate to criminal syndicate), are also spreading throughout civil society due to their facility of use, portability, and durability.

As accessibility to new and more powerful weaponry makes it easier to kill people, it is easier for countries to be locked in perpetual cycles of (internal) conflict that render any 'normal' trajectory of political and economic development impossible. This has increased the virulence of mass violence (e.g. fatality rates) as automatic rifles are replacing single-action and non-automatic weapons. But the majority of casualties are young men, often unemployed and with limited formal education. The early death or injury of productive individuals obviously affects the production capacities of entire societies, exerting tremendous strains on public health facilities.

The targeting of civilians in situations of war, regardless of whether they are men, women or children, constitutes a grave violation of international humanitarian law. The availability of small arms, then, constitutes a threat to basic human rights such as the right to life, liberty, and security of person (Art. 3, UN Declaration of Human Rights). But the impact of small arms is not restricted to death and injury.

Evidence gathered suggests that arms often play a vital role in compelling people to leave their homes. The global caseload of refugees and displaced persons, a proxy indicator of armed violence, is growing. The number of refugees fleeing from armed conflicts worldwide increased from 2.4 million in 1974 to more than 27.4 million by the year 2000, with another 23 million people internally displaced.[11] Children and women make up an estimated 70–80 per cent of displaced populations. Violence-induced displacement inhibits the access of vulnerable groups to education and health, resulting in long-term costs to social well-being and economic activity more generally.

While the presence of small arms and light weapons progressively undermines the very existence of the State, persistent armed violence limits the capacity of States to create responsive institutions that are critical to ensuring prosperity, safety, and social welfare. What is more, access of civilians to public goods and services is severely constrained by the widespread availability and use of weapons.

Additionally, war-related agricultural declines often have disastrous consequences. Global economic losses from unrelenting armed conflict in developing countries over the past two decades amount to an estimated US $37 billion, while those states received only US $29 billion in food aid over the same period.[12]

[11] UNHCR figures for the year 2000.

[12] Natalie Goldring, 'Links between Domestic Laws and International Light Weapons Control', Project on Light Weapons, British–American Security Information Council (BASIC) Publications, 11–12 December 1997, p. 27.

Though small arms are but one of the many factors that contribute to these gross impacts, the long-term macroeconomic costs are staggering, reducing economic productivity and severely distorting the cost of living.

In many parts of the world where armed conflicts show no sign of abating, development gains are severely curtailed due to the destruction of human capital, infrastructure, inflation and the perceived risks associated with long-term investment. Relief operations and implementing partners are habitually paralysed by armed violence, with humanitarian agencies often forced to evacuate or devote resources to capital and logistics-intensive emergency assistance.

THE POST-9/11 SECURITY DISCOURSE

In many ways, 11 September (9/11) was an epochal event which has altered the security discourse in the international system and changed the structure of this system itself. As detailed earlier, during the post-Cold War era, the State had begun to lose its pre-eminence as being the principal actor in the structure of international security. Globalization, regionalization and economic liberalization had diluted the State's sphere of influence and replaced it with transnational institutions and supranational organizations. While State-centric military security was relegated to a secondary position, human security, encompassing a wider discourse on security, took centre stage.

However, with 9/11, the State has regained its primacy within the larger security debate. How can the State attempt to provide adequate human security when its very existence is being challenged by terrorist activity? Therefore, the focus of security shifted again from being human-centric to State-centric. And this has come about by elevating 'terrorism', a predominantly non-traditional threat to security, to the magnitude of a military threat; 'war against terrorism' may not be just a coincidental coinage.

That the State has regained its primacy in the security debate is apparent from some of the counter-terror measures adopted by the states post-9/11. There has been a visible trend towards regaining the authority of the State in more militaristic terms. Take the case of South Asia, for example: the year-long Indian border mobilization, despite its underlying danger of drifting into conventional conflict that could acquire a nuclear dimension, was catalysed by and reflective of the changed international security situation. In Pakistan, the military regime strengthened its position by altering the Constitution to its advantage. The legal changes brought about in the Constitution have eroded the authority of the prime minister *vis-à-vis* the president and established a secure role for the military to guide the democratic process in Pakistan. In Nepal, the Maoists were branded as terrorists for the first time, with the army being deployed for counter-terror operations. Following 11 September, China has equated the Muslim separatists in Xinjiang with terrorists during the course of a meeting of the Shanghai Cooperation Organization on terrorism. These are subtle but concrete changes that underline the growing authority of the State. Ironically, though the discourse has shifted once again to State security, it is human security that is at stake.

HUMAN SECURITY OR STATE SECURITY?

How do we locate the issue of small arms in this evolving scenario? The proliferation of small arms affects the State even when viewed within the narrow concept of State security or studied through the comprehensive paradigm of human security. State security and human security are the thresholds of the security debate and it is unlikely that any future debate can go beyond these two points. Either way, the proliferation of small arms is a threat to security—exclusive State security or inclusive human security.

CHAPTER 2

The Problem of Small Arms in South Asia

With an estimated 500–700 million small arms in circulation (of which nearly 1 per cent are held illicitly), coupled with nearly half a million deaths resulting from small arms (90 per cent of which pertain to unarmed civilians), the issue needs no advocacy. Like money laundering, small arms have permeated and become a crucial link in all known criminal and terrorist activity. Unfortunately, while governments have woken up to the dangers of money laundering and enacted appropriate national, regional, and international legislation, the problem of small arms continues to be looked at in isolation, or *in tandem* with conflicts, rather than being identified and associated with criminal or terrorist activity.

THE CASE OF PAKISTAN

In the case of South Asia, and, more specifically, Pakistan, some very interesting aspects come to light. The sources of weapons supply and acquisition have been myriad, ranging from illicit influx, transfer or trade to local production facilities. Several countries in the region produce small arms and light weapons in government-owned or public enterprises, which are lawfully regulated, with India and Pakistan supporting the most developed weapons manufacturing capacities. But the predominant form of acquisition of light weapons by the state security forces continues to be import or foreign technology transfer.

In Pakistan, the problem of small arms is not limited to proliferation and illegal production, but results from prevailing gun culture and a legacy of conflicts. The scourge of small arms proliferation affects all countries of South Asia to varying degrees, but Pakistan has been the hardest hit with the largest concentration of weapons, its source being the CIA-sponsored arms pipeline to the Afghan fighting militia through Pakistan in the 1980s, and the frontier region of Pakistan or the Darra Bara, commonly known as the 'Main Open Arms Bazaar'.

In a study conducted on the pilferage and trafficking of small arms, Brig. Shahedul Anam Khan regards the end of the Cold War and the transformation of the world order as the main causes behind the easy flow, availability, and trade of these weapons at illicit level.[1] The reason is that in this transitory phase, Europe, North America and Asia unveiled their huge arms stockpiles, creating a glut in the world arms market of used but quite modern weapons. This gradually put pressure on cash-poor countries (such as the former Soviet Union and Eastern European countries) to sell their surplus. Not all of these transactions, however, were done officially. Arms were also sold illegally, ensuring light-weapons delivery around the world through the black market, secret government-to-government deals, and the sponsorship of substate groups.

The motives for which suppliers and recipients engage in transfers may be mixed. Suppliers may have a political agenda or commercial motives or a mix of the two. With particular reference to Pakistan, the predominant form of acquisition of weapons by security forces as well as by Non-State Actors (NSA) has been through the following means:

1. Imports or foreign technology transfers.[2]
2. The availability of light weapons in other parts of South Asia

[1] Brig. Shahedul Anam Khan, 'Linkages between Arms Trafficking and the Drug Trade in South Asia', in *Small Arms Control: Old Weapons, New Issues*, ed. Lora Lumpe, UNIDIR, Aldershot: Ashgate Publishing, 1999, p. 178.

[2] Lora Lumpe, 'Leader of the Pack', *The Bulletin of the Atomic Scientists*, January/February 1999, pp. 27–33; 'Recycled Weapons: American Exports of Surplus Weapons, 1990–1995', *Report Prepared for the Federation of Atomic Scientists*, Washington, D.C., 1996. The author has discussed in detail the US Foreign Assistance Act and its active, material support to allied warring actors during covert operations.

partly reflects the onward shipment of weapons originally intended for use in Afghanistan.

3. A major source of weapons purchase, proliferation, and production is the centuries-old Darra Bara, which was once regarded as a cottage industry but has now become a huge industrial enterprise, but free of government control and taxation policies. The private gun-manufacturing units of Darra have a production capacity of not less than a hundred AK-47s per day. Proud of their skill, the gunsmiths of Darra Adam Khel (DAK) and Landi Kotal, as well as those scattered around Peshawar, certain parts of Baluchistan, and Afghanistan, are proficient enough to manufacture any kind of sophisticated firearms, which are much cheaper.[3]
4. The Soviet invasion of Afghanistan in December 1979 ushered in a new era in the light weapons trade in South Asia. Other interested parties also contributed directly and indirectly to the *mujahideen*, such as China (weaponry) and Saudi Arabia (financing). Pakistan became the conduit for this massive military assistance programme, with the Central Intelligence Agency (CIA) coordinating the supply of weapons and the Pakistani Inter-Services Intelligence (ISI) responsible for receipt and distribution.[4]

Since the end of the Afghan war, the availability of arms on the commercial market has increased considerably and in some cases prices have fallen. For one thing, many Afghans returning to their

[3] For a detailed study of Darra gunsmiths and the impact of light weapons on Pakistani society, see Ayesha Agha, 'Arresting Light Weapons Proliferation in South Asia: Is there a Way Ahead?', in *Over A Barrel, Light Weapons and Human Rights in the Commonwealth*, ed. Abdel-Fatau Musah and Niobe Thompson, London: Commonwealth Human Rights Initiative (CHRI), 2000. Also see by Agha, 'Light Weapons Manufacture in the Public and Private Sectors: A View From Pakistan', in *Project on Light Weapons*, BASIC Working Paper No. 2, London: British–American Security Information Council (BASIC) Publications, 1996.

[4] Chris Smith, 'Light Weapons and Ethnic Conflict in South Asia', in *Lethal Commerce: The Global Trade in Small Arms and Light Weapons*, ed. Jeffery Boutwell and Michael T. Klare, Cambridge, MA: American Academy of Arts and Sciences, pp. 62–3.

country after months or years in refugee camps in the NWFP left their weapons behind in Pakistan.

Based on these sources, the various weapons on sale fall into four categories:

- First, there are weapons that leaked from the US-supported arms pipeline. Following the Geneva Accords, which effectively marked the withdrawal of Soviet occupational forces, US arms supplies actually increased to ensure a Soviet withdrawal. All of these systems, notably Stingers, remained in the region after the Soviet withdrawal. In spite of the US government's Buy-Back initiative at the end of the Soviet occupation, from the Afghan *jihadi* groups, the entire stock of Stingers was not fully recovered or traceable;
- Second, are the stocks of Soviet weapons captured by the *mujahideen* during the conflict;
- Third, are those manufactured by the small-scale producers within the region. They include both the Darra private gun manufacturers and the State-licenced and regulated public arms producers; and
- Last, are the arms bazaars of the NWFP which are full of miscellaneous weapons that arrive in the region through extremely circuitous routes—from Vietnam or the Middle East.[5]

Today, it is widely recognized that Afghanistan is the world's leading centre for unaccounted for weapons, with at least 10 million in circulation within the country. The Afghan war against the Soviet Union was long and brutal, as was the civil war that followed. Even so, it is not easy to reconcile such an estimate with a total population of only about seven million Afghan men aged 18 to 52, especially considering that this figure also includes millions of Afghan men still living in Iran and Pakistan.

The superpowers, China, and their allies delivered large quantities of light weapons ranging from landmines to surface-to-air missiles. These deliveries were mainly to non-State combatants in civil and regional conflicts throughout the Cold War. Throughout

[5] Ibid.

much of the Cold War, the US government engaged in covert political and military operations, including secret arms supply to state and guerrilla forces, authorized under the National Security Act of 1947.[6] The US policy of arming the *mujahideen* is best explained by Lora Lumpe:

> The Reagan Government's Afghan policy emphasized arming multiple resistance groups known collectively as mujahideen in order to draw [the] Soviet Union into a costly and damaging war for control of Afghanistan. This case is unique among the Reagan Doctrine cases in that the administration and the CIA had an unambiguous green light from Congress to arm the insurgents. As a result, the full extent of the program did not require concealment, as was the case with arms supply to groups in Angola, Cambodia and Nicaragua. Unlike the latter cases, which used covert delivery systems to hide war making from Congress and the public, the arms pipeline to Afghanistan relied on channels with little accountability because of preconditions set by the intelligence and military services within Pakistan which served as the primary staging ground for the fighting groups and which did not want to be seen as engaging in direct confrontation with the Soviet Union.[7]

The *mujahideen* already had access to the arms they had pilfered from the Democratic Republic of Afghanistan (DRA) and Soviet stocks and small amounts supplied through China or the Pakistani pipeline. Significant external supply began in 1985–6, which primarily aided the *mujahideen* to wage a ground war against air attacks. By 1988, the *mujahideen* arsenal reportedly included AK-47s, AK-74s, SKS 7.62 mm. rifles, Iranian 7.62 mm. G3 rifles, 9 mm. Sten guns, shotguns, Chinese-made Type 56-1 assault rifles, and light machine guns (7.62 mm. RPD and RPK, the 7.62 mm. PKM, and older Czech weapons).

Lora Lumpe also debunks the popularly held theory regarding the *mujahideen's* use of missiles, particularly Stingers. According to her, various varieties of missiles were already in use by the *mujahideen* before Stingers arrived. Initially, the US supplies were

[6] Lucy Mathiak and Lora Lumpe, 'Govt. Gun Running to Guerrillas', in *Running Guns*, ed. Lora Lumpe, London: Zed Books, 2000, pp. 56–67.

[7] Ibid., pp. 57–8.

restricted to replicas of Soviet weaponry, such as SAM-7 and SAM-9; these shipments were arranged through various routes such as Turkey or Egypt in order to further mask US involvement.[8] China, acting in its own interest in countering Soviet influence, eventually emerged as the main supplier of missiles to the guerrillas over the course of the war.[9] Therefore, the Afghans had been using a range of surface-to-air missiles long before the first 150 Stingers arrived in the summer of 1986, which represented only a small proportion of the missiles they employed to counter Soviet airpower.[10] Because of the controversy behind the supply of Stinger missiles, particularly the opposition from the CIA, the quantity of missiles and the chain of transfer was relatively restricted. After the Soviet withdrawal, the Stingers were allegedly used in other conflicts, and ultimately became the focus of a highly publicized but futile US effort to recover the missiles.

The situation in Pakistan got exacerbated not only because of the US policy to arm the Afghan rebels, but also particularly because Pakistan was being used as the primary conduit to transfer the weapons to the conflict zone. In general, weapons and other military equipment intended for resistance groups were included in the military modernization packages for primary conduit states, which were expected to send their obsolete and overstocked equipment to the respective groups. While a portion of such weapons did make it to the intended recipients, sufficient leakage in this pipeline can also be traced as members of conduit state militaries often took advantage of such surpluses by entering the lucrative black market.[11] Pakistan can be cited as a case in point.

Pakistan emerged as the fourth-largest recipient of US aid in exchange for its role as an arms conduit to the *mujahideen*. During

[8] US Department of State cable. Egypt also included other weapons, such as shoulder-fired AT and anti-aircraft rockets, guns and ammunition: 'Aid to Afghanistan Insurgents', 2 June 1980.

[9] Anthony H. Cordesman and Abraham R. Wagner, *Lessons of Modern War*, vol. III: *The Afghan and the Falklands Conflicts*, Boulder, CO: Westview Press, 1999, pp. 172–3, as quoted in Lumpe, *Running Guns*.

[10] Lumpe, *Running Guns*, p. 58.

[11] Ibid.

1980, the US Congress appropriated $30 million in covert programmes intended to directly aid the *mujahideen*, and $1.5 billion in overt military and other aid for the government of Pakistan in exchange for playing this role. Pakistan is the only country bordering Afghanistan through which the US could arrange arms shipments to the Afghan resistance, and, at the same time, Pakistan had legitimate security concerns because of developments in Afghanistan. As a result of the Soviet invasion, in late September 1980 there were reportedly not less than 200 violations of Pakistan's airspace by the Soviets.[12]

Pakistan's ISI demanded and got control over the arms pipeline and the choice of recipients as a precondition for the country's help in channelling weapons to the *mujahideen*. Control over the supply lines gave the ISI enviable access to vast stores of weapons. Between 1979 and 1989, the CIA channelled $2 billion in weapons aid, or an estimated 80 per cent of the agency's covert aid budget, to the *mujahideen*. The ISI used its role in the pipeline and appropriated between 50–70 per cent of the military resources intended for the *mujahideen* for its own purposes. The agency and its partners used the diverted weapons for self-aggrandizement through black market sales. They also retained a portion of the weapons to consolidate their own power within Pakistan's military and civil society. The diversions came to the notice of the US, but it decided to ignore them as 'unpleasant but necessary element[s] of the aid programme'.[13]

Added to the glut of weapons within Pakistan due to the wanton leakage in the weapons pipeline, the ISI's policy of arming select resistance groups within the *mujahideen* had further repercussions for Pakistan's security. Under ISI management, most of the aid went to the six main *mujahideen* groups based in Peshawar, known as the 'Peshawar groups', led by Hekmatyar and Rabbani. Just as the ISI skimmed a large percentage of the aid off the

[12] Richard P. Cronin, 'Pakistan: US Foreign Assistance Facts', *Congressional Research Services Issue Brief 85112*, 20 July 1987, p. 1; Diego Cordovez and Selig Harrison, *Out of Afghanistan: The Inside Story of the Soviet Withdrawal*, New York: Oxford University Press, 1995, pp. 54–8.

[13] Lumpe, *Running Guns*, p. 62.

top, these groups also diverted and stockpiled a portion of the weapons for use in enforcing their respective ideologies.[14]

Lora Lumpe notes: 'Thus, there were three disparate sets of interests at work in the US–Pakistan–Afghanistan triangle. Just as Pakistan's security interests differed in perspectives and practice from those of the US, the ideological objectives of the Peshawar groups varied dramatically from those of either Pakistan or the United States.'[15] As a result of the stockpiling of weapons by these private parties, the conflict extended endlessly despite the discontinuation of external weapons support some time later.

The region most directly affected by the growing availability of small arms and light weapons has been the province of Sind and its state capital Karachi. Though the problems in Sind have been more political than ideological, many divisions have occurred along ethnic lines. Throughout the 1980s, violence in Karachi reached unprecedented and shocking levels prior to the Pakistan Army's intervention in 1992. Although Sind displays a violent streak, several analysts from Karachi agree that the dramatic increase in the violence and polarization dates from 1985 to 1986, when weapons from the Afghan pipeline began to find their way into commercial channels.

Ayesha Agha in one of her studies, pinpoints several factors that have affected and in turn been adversely hit by small arms proliferation:[16]

1. Ethnic divisions and bad governance;
2. Rise in sectarianism, coupled with the mushrooming of religious schools that took sectarian ideology to the grass-roots level, enhancing dogmatic orthodoxy;
3. Lack of social and human development accompanying the fragmentation of Pakistan's Muslim society;
4. Systematic judicial corruption;
5. Very adversely affected economic indicators;

[14] 'The United States, Pakistan and the Soviet Threat to South Asia', *Congressional Research Service Report No. 85–152F*, September 1985, pp. 23–4.

[15] Lumpe, *Running Guns*, p. 64.

[16] Agha, 'Arresting Light Weapons', in *Over a Barrel*.

6. The additional factor of fragmentation of Afghanistan, the rise of the Taliban movement, which was followed by the Islamization of arms transfer;[17] and
7. The appeasement policies adopted by the political leadership, such as awarding various alliance group members with prohibited-bore licences.

The weaponization of the North-West Frontier Province (NWFP) is legendary, as is the level of gun violence in Lahore. The difficulty of establishing stable civilian rule is clear in Pakistan, where the 1999 coup by General Musharraf provides a recent demonstration of the ways in which covert arms supply operations have often undermined civil society and democratic development in partner countries.[18] The Afghan pipeline contributed not only to an ongoing humanitarian crisis and to state and regional instability, but it also strengthened a global network of fundamentalist, virulently anti-Western, and, in particular, anti-American sentiment. But the rot did not stop just there.

The problem for Pakistan did not stem from just the US Afghan policy. It had its roots in the Afghan *jihad* perpetrated by the US with the aim of isolating Iran. The Afghan *jihad* eventually resulted in the Islamization of the Pakistani society. Hatred bred through these *jihads* was manifest in violent ways due to easy access to small arms made available, again, by the Afghan policy of the US.

The *jihad* facilitated the recruitment of radical Muslims from around the world to train in Pakistan and fight with the Afghan *mujahideen*. It was in this context that the US-Saudi-Pakistani alliance was forged, and religious *madrasas* were turned into political schools for training cadres. With Pakistan already a willing partner and a conduit for arms to the *mujahideen*, the CIA advertised for, and openly recruited, Islamic holy warriors from Egypt, Saudi Arabia, Sudan, and Algeria. The CIA looked for but

[17] Pyotr G. Litvarin, 'Sources of Small Arms and Light Weapons Procurement in Southwest Asia', in *Small Arms, Big Impact: The Next Challenge of Disarmament*, ed. Michael Renner, Washington, D.C : Worldwatch Press, 1997.

[18] Lumpe, *Running Guns*, p. 64.

was unable to find a Saudi prince to lead this crusade. It settled for the next best thing; the son of an illustrious family closely connected to the Saudi royal house—Osama bin Laden. Laden was recruited with US approval and, at the highest level, by Prince Turki al-Faisal, the then head of Saudi intelligence. This is the background in which Osama bin Laden helped build the Khost tunnel complex deep under the mountains close to the Pakistani border in 1986, a complex the CIA funded as a major arms depot, as a training facility, and as a medical centre for the *mujahideen*. It was also the background in which bin Laden set up 'Al-Qaeda' ('the base') in 1989 as a service centre for Arab Afghans and their families. The idea of an Islamic global war was not the brainchild of bin Laden: the CIA and Pakistan's ISI hoped to transform the Afghan *jihad* into a global war waged by Muslim states against the Soviet Union.

The US and Saudi Arabia funnelled some $3.5 billion into Afghanistan and Pakistan during the Afghan war, according to Milt Bearden, CIA station chief in Pakistan from 1986 to 1989. '*Jihad*', along with guns and drugs, became the most important business in the region.

The *jihad* movement now continues with its own financial momentum that it has come to acquire, and it has become increasingly difficult for Pakistan to shut it down.[19] Writing in *Foreign Affairs*, Ahmad Rashid estimated that 35,000 Muslim radicals from 40 Islamic countries joined Afghanistan's fight in the decade 1982–92. Eventually, Rashid notes, the Afghan *jihad* came to influence more than 100,000 foreign Muslim radicals.

The Afghan *jihad* was the largest covert operation in the history of the CIA. In fiscal 1987 alone, according to one estimate, clandestine US military aid to the *mujahideen* amounted to 660 million dollars. Apart from direct US funding, the CIA financed the war through the drug trade. The impact on Afghanistan and Pakistan was devastating. Prior to the Afghan *jihad*, there was no local production of heroin in Pakistan and Afghanistan:

[19] Jessica Stern, 'Pakistan's Jihad Culture', *Foreign Affairs*, vol. 70, no. 6, November/December 2000, pp. 115–26.

the production of opium was directed to small regional markets. Michel Chossudovsky, Professor of Economics at the University of Ottawa, estimates that within only two years of the CIA's entry into the Afghan *jihad*, 'the Pakistan-Afghanistan borderlands became the world's top heroin producer, supplying 60 per cent of US demand'.[20] By the end of the anti-Soviet *jihad*, the Central Asian region produced 75 per cent of the world's opium, worth billions of dollars in revenue.

To begin with, the increase in opium production corresponded to an increase in local consumption. The UN Drug Control Programme estimated that the heroin-addicted population in Pakistan went up from nearly zero in 1979 to 1.2 million by 1985.

There were two other ways in which the Afghan *jihad* affected Pakistan. The first was its impact on Pakistan's military and intelligence services, which were the key to the CIA gaining an effective reach in Afghanistan and, more generally, in Soviet Central Asia. The more the anti-Soviet *jihad* grew, the more the intelligence services, particularly the ISI, moved to the centre of governmental power in Pakistan. The Islamization of the anti-Soviet struggle drew inspiration from and reinforced the Islamization of the Pakistani State under General Zia. Second, the more momentum the Afghan *jihad* gathered, the more it fed a regional offshoot, the Kashmiri *jihad*. The *jihadi* organizations were pivotal in the functioning of the Pakistani State by the time Zia left office, and the trend of Islamization of the State continued by post-Zia governments as well.

The impact of these factors on the overall societal growth and human security aspect of the Pakistani society was extremely negative. The rising sectarian, dogmatic orthodoxy, coupled with easy access to and unfettered use of firearms, besides instilling deep-rooted fears in the masses brought Pakistan close to being labelled a terrorist state.

Apart from the deluge of weapons from the Afghan conundrum, Chris Smith points out the Pakistan Ordnance Factories

[20] Michel Chossudovsky, 'Osamagate', Centre for Research on Globalization (CRG), October 2001: http://globalresearch.ca/articles/CHO110A.html.

(POF) as a possible source, but the likelihood of any pilferage is very low given the stringent control measures enforced. The POF at Wah, is a State-owned weapons manufacturer which was established in 1950 after partition from India. The main idea behind the establishment of the POF was to make the country self-sufficient in small arms and ammunition production. It now comprises 14 plants and 8 subsidiary companies and employs more than 30,000 people.[21] The company manufactures a wide range of weapons, most of which are produced under licence, including small arms and ammunition as well as medium and heavy artillery and AT weapons. In 1986, the company reportedly employed some 40,000 people and had military exports of $30–35 million annually, with a stated goal of $150 million per year in the near future.[22] The small arms manufactured under licenced production agreements include Heckler & Koch's G3A3 and G3A4 assault rifles, MP5A2 and A3 sub-machine guns and P7M13 pistols. In addition, the POF reportedly manufactures Rheinmetall MG3 machine guns and Royal Ordnance Factories' 105 mm. AT ammunition as well as anti-personnel landmines.[23] The POF has exported arms to a number of countries such as France, Morocco, Sri Lanka, the Gulf States, the Philippines National Police, Kenya, South Africa, and even to the repressive Myanmar (Burmese) junta.[24]

All of these items are produced under licence with a very stringent control mechanism and maintenance of complete records. The items thus produced are not only ISO 9001 certified, but are also governed by strict export regulations under the government's Statutory Regulatory Orders (SRO 123/124 of February 1998). Of these two, SRO 124 in particular makes it mandatory for the POF to obtain a No Objection Certificate (NOC) from the

[21] GIIS, 'Half a Billion', *The Small Arms Survey*, p. 43.

[22] 'POF: The Hidden Giant', *Military Technology*, vol. 10, no. 9, September 1986, pp. S62–7.

[23] 'Episcope: 100 mm APFSDS Ammunition from POF', *Heracles*, no. 53, August 1986, p. 6.

[24] 'POF and Fax Communication', *Far Eastern Economic Review*, 15 November 1990, p. 95.

Defence Production Division of the Ministry of Defence, which is in addition to the clearances sought from the Ministry of Foreign Affairs and the Director Arms Control, Strategic Arms Division. The NOC is for the export of arms, ammunition, explosives, and ingredients thereof, as well as complete rocket and Unmanned Aerial Vehicles (UAV) and their parts. And through the NOC it is ensured that the permits being issued are not for non-State forces and/or conflict zones.[25]

As such not a profit-based entity, the principal reason behind establishing the POF was to provide the Pakistani military with a weapons production facility so that its dependence on foreign sources was minimized. Thus, as mentioned above, the revenue generation criterion does not find much relevance in this case. The point to be noted here is that due to a limited demand, the POF's full production capacity is not being properly utilized. Thus, the factories end up producing only what is required by the principal client, the Pakistani military, and this, of course, is quite restricted in scope given the ammunitions production capacity, which is not more than $70 million.[26]

Besides producing armaments for the Pakistan military, in the last decade or so, the POF has also entered into licenced production agreements with a few countries of which agreements with German arms manufacturing firms are the most important.[27] Through licenced production agreements, the POF either 'buys' a contract, or provides end-user certification to such arms shipments. According to Lora Lumpe in *Running Guns*:

> In a 1992 interview, a Pakistani arms manufacturer was surprisingly frank in revealing one reason for establishing licenced production agreements with POF. According to him, POF, which had long maintained ties with

[25] Iffat S. Malik, 'Countering Small Arms and Light Weapons Proliferation in South Asia', in *South Asia at Gun Point, Small Arms and Light Weapons Proliferation*, ed. Dipankar Banerji, New Delhi: Manohar and Regional Centre for Strategic Studies, 2000, p. 242.

[26] Agha, 'Arresting Light Weapons', in *Over a Barrel*, p. 4.

[27] 'Pak. Serves as German Arms Export Front', *Middle East Defence News—Technology Watch*, 20 January 1992, p. 95.

German arms manufacturers, had recently begun providing a new service, end use certificates to cover German shipments to Kuwait. Arms exports to [the] Middle East are illegal under German law, and have frequently aroused controversy. By going through Pakistan, a legal destination, many German companies had found a convenient route to enter the Middle East market. Some of Germany's largest weapons manufacturers had granted production licenses to the POF, so sales to Pakistan did not raise problems in Bonn. The article also described another variation of the end-user scheme in which German companies would negotiate a contract with a Middle Eastern client, then hand it to POF for the actual deliveries, in essence 'selling' their contract to the Pakistanis.[28]

From 1960 to 1999, 14 countries established small arms and ammunition licenced production agreements with some 46 countries.[29] A 1995 report estimated that licenced production was taking place in at least 21 developing countries; 16 of them were also exporting the small arms they manufactured. These countries included Brazil, Chile, Egypt, India, Indonesia, Iran, North and South Korea, Pakistan, Singapore, South Africa, and Turkey.[30] But all of these productions and exports are legal and function under strict governmental and international regulations.

The illegal production of the small arms in circulation in large numbers is dealt with in detail in the following chapter which highlights the problem of illegal production and calls for international attention to this ignored aspect of weapons proliferation.

[28] Lumpe, *Running Guns*, pp. 88–9.

[29] Ibid., p. 88. The 14 licensing States are: Austria, Belgium, the Czech Republic, France, Germany, Israel, Italy, Portugal, South Africa, Singapore, Sweden, Switzerland, the United Kingdom and the United States of America. The 46 licensees are: Argentina, Australia, Belgium, Brazil, Bulgaria, Burma, Canada, Chile, China, Colombia, the Czech Republic, Egypt, France, Germany, Greece, India, Indonesia, Iran, Iraq, Italy, Japan, Kenya, Malaysia, Mexico, Morocco, Nigeria, Norway, North Korea, Pakistan, the Philippines, Poland, Portugal, Romania, Saudi Arabia, Singapore, South Korea, Spain, Sweden, Switzerland, Taiwan, Thailand, Turkey, the United Kingdom, the United States of America, former Yugoslavia, and Venezuela.

[30] M. Klare, 'Light Weapons Diffusion', in *Light Weapons and International Security*, ed. Jasjit Singh, New Delhi: Pugwash Conferences on Science and World Affairs, 1995.

THE CASE OF SRI LANKA

The Sri Lankan crisis or its perpetrator, the LTTE, needs no introduction. Despite a long history of discontent and hatred fuelled by incumbent governments, the issue precipitated with the Eelam wars waged in the last two decades. The presence of small arms and light weapons has exacerbated the situation. The conflict has caused about 65,000 deaths, a whopping two-thirds of which are of innocent civilians.[31] Development and civic infrastructure have been totally destroyed, turning back the development clock in the north-east region by about two decades. The wars have wrecked the island State economically, socially, militarily, and politically. Extensive use of small arms and light weapons by both parties has contributed to this.

According to Rohan Gunaratna:

> The LTTE procured and employed weapons in the lower end of the small arms spectrum until early 1984...[t]he ethnic constituency pressure from Tamil Nadu and geographical differences between New Delhi and Colombo, changed the complex of the conflict. Although [the] Research and Analysis Wing (RAW), India's foreign intelligence agency, provided training and weapons to the LTTE from November 1983, it was cautious not to provide them with stand-off weapons such as RPGs, LAWs and SAMs. But the LTTE, bent on self-reliance, developed an independent international arms procurement network since early 1984.[32]

Gunaratna explains that the Tigers' drive to procure stand-off weapons stemmed from the huge losses they suffered during the battle for Elephant Pass in 1991: they realized that their losses were primarily because of the lack of a stand-off capability. 'Since 1991, LTTE procurement patterns indicate that the LTTE has been focusing on building a stand-off capability.'[33] By 1997, it achieved its objective through a successful heist of 34,500 mortars (81 mm.) and a consignment of MBRLs (Multi-Barrel Rocket Launchers) from Serbia.[34]

[31] Chris Smith, 'In the Shadow of a Ceasefire: The Impacts of Small Arms Availability and Misuse in Sri Lanka', *Small Arms Survey Occasional Paper No. 11*, October 2003, p. 1.

[32] Rohan Gunaratna, 'Sources of Arms Supplies to the LTTE: Success and Failure of the Sri Lankan State in Meeting the Threat', in Banerjee, *South Asia at Gun Point*.

[33] Ibid.

[34] Ibid.

The LTTE has been able to obtain its weapons independent of external support through its large support base spread all over the world. Excluding contributions from the US, where a ban on raising money for organizations branded as 'terrorist organizations' is in place, the LTTE is able to collect US $1 million each month from the Tamil expatriates in Australia, Canada, Switzerland and the UK.[35] In addition to the monies obtained through collection from the Tamil diaspora, the LTTE has also established a whole range of businesses that generate income. It has its own fleet of ocean-going ships referred to as 'Sea Pigeons', which normally carry legitimate cargo and ferry weapons for the LTTE whenever there is a need. The LTTE owns at least 11 small freighters which are involved in this activity.[36]

The LTTE has managed to obtain its weapons from a variety of souices. In the mid-1980s, Singapore remained an important source of arms, particularly for dual-use items. In the mid-1990s, the LLTE also obtained large quantities of weapons from Cambodia, including surface-to-air missiles (SAM-7s).[37] This was in addition to tapping the glut of weapons flooding the black markets following the end of the Cold War and from conflict zones in Africa.

The LTTE has also been successful in obtaining large quantities of weapons and explosives from their ambushes and raids against the Sri Lankan Army units; it is believed that the LTTE has accumulated about 10,000 weapons through such means, and 80–90 per cent of personal weapons carried by the LTTE are from these raids.[38] Also, each member is said to possess at least two assault rifles.[39]

The Sri Lankan Army and the LTTE are not the only armed sections within the Sri Lankan society. Large quantities of arms are also present with other State agencies like the Home Guards (shotguns), National Armed Reserve/National Guard (79,000

[35] Smith, 'In the Shadow of a Ceasefire'.

[36] Daniel Byman, Peter Chalk, Bruce Hoffman, William Rosenau, and David Brannan, *Trends in Outside Support for Insurgent Movements*, Santa Monica: RAND, 2001, as quoted in Smith, 'In the Shadow of a Ceasefire', p. 10.

[37] Smith, 'In the Shadow of a Ceasefire', p. 11.

[38] Gunaratna, 'Sources of Arms Supplies', p. 66.

[39] Smith, 'In the Shadow of a Ceasefire', p. 13.

small arms), police (34,000 small arms), in addition to registered and unregistered stockpiles. According to a guesstimate by the *Small Arms Survey* (2002), there could be up to 1,900,000 civilian firearms. Added to the problem is the high rate of desertion in the Sri Lankan Army, with some soldiers leaving with the weapons issued to them.

The effects of such a huge volume of weapons in the hands of combatants and civilians are not hard to discern. The immediate consequence of the violent conflict has been widespread death and destruction. This had triggered an exodus of people to neighbouring India, as well as to many developed countries. There is also large-scale displacement within the island State. In the conflict zones, the economic infrastructure has collapsed leading to and resulting from the disruption in economic activities established earlier. The psychological impact of being trapped in unending violence has been devastating. Sri Lanka has the highest rate of suicides; with over 55 suicides per 100,000 persons, it is more than double the world average of 25 per 100,000.[40] Coupled with all this is the plight of humanitarian agencies, which find it difficult to ameliorate the current situation because of the ceaseless armed violence.

THE CASE OF INDIA

Unlike Pakistan, where excess supply is generating a demand, in the case of India a huge demand for weapons exists due to various insurgencies and armed conflicts in various degrees of intensity in many areas of the country. Straddled between two zones (Afghanistan and South-East Asia) awash with weapons, it is not difficult for NSAs to dip into the black market either on their own or with help from external sources.

KASHMIR

In Jammu & Kashmir, there are at least a hundred militant groups in operation. Though most of these groups are minor and basically splinter groups, in some instances having only one member,

[40] Ibid., p. 19.

almost all have arms ranging from grenades to AK-47s. Among this multitude of groups, three are prominent: (i) Hizbul Mujahideen; whose cadres are mostly Kashmiris and whose strength in the Valley is estimated to be around 800; (ii) Harkat-ul Mujahideen; whose cadres are mostly Afghans and of a total strength of 5,000 cadres, 350 are operating in Jammu & Kashmir. The Harkat-ul Mujahideen was earlier known as the Harkat-ul-Ansar; it rechristened itself after the US declared it a terrorist group in 1997; and (iii) Lashkar-e-Toiba (LeT) which has about 300 cadres operating in Kashmir. The LeT is the militant wing of the Markaz Dawa-ul-Arshad, which is located in Muridke, 30 km north of Lahore (Pakistan). The magnitude of foreign terrorists is indeed a unique and later development in Jammu & Kashmir. The statistics given in Table 2.1 reveal that there were virtually no foreign terrorists in the Valley in the earlier stages of the conflict. Now, however,

TABLE 2.1: LIST OF FOREIGN TERRORISTS KILLED

Year	Total terrorists killed by the security forces in J&K	Foreign terrorists killed by the security forces	Foreign terrorists killed per centage of the total terrorists killed	Total terrorists surrendered to security forces
2004*	455	303	66.59	68
2003	1,447	1,004	69.38	119
2002	1,707	1,063	62.3	159
2001	2,020	1,198	58.8	85
2000	1,520	870	53.9	104
1999	1,082	548	50.6	109
1998	999	406	40.6	187
1997	1,075	260	24.2	270
1996	1,209	213	17.6	655
1995	1,332	77	5.7	601
1994	1,596	77	4.8	32
1993	1,310	79	6.0	98
1992	819	6	0.73	444
1991	844	2	0.2	612
1990	550	0	0.0	0
Total	17,965	6,106	–	3,543

Note: * Up to 30 June 2004.

Source: http://www.armyinkashmir.org/v2/statistical_facts/ft_actual_data.shtml

more foreign terrorists are being apprehended and killed by the Indian security forces, and they constitute as many as 70 per cent of the militants operating there.

As mentioned earlier, there is no dearth of weapons for the terrorists operating in Jammu & Kashmir. They are the first groups of terrorists in the country to have access to sophisticated weapons and explosives. Since they hold no territory like the LTTE, their supply of weapons has been restricted to small arms and light weapons, and no large-scale acquisitions of stand-off heavy weaponry and mortars have been made. The statistics of weapons seized from the militants in Jammu & Kashmir as given in Table 2.2 are indicative of the range and quantity of weapons in the possession of the militants. Needless to say, this represents only a fraction of the quality of weapons stockpiled by the militants.

Analysis of the statistics also reveals an increased use of explosives corresponding to an overall decrease in assault weapons. This is so because of the established advantages explosive devices have over weapons in the latest tactics being adopted by the terrorists. The reasons why explosive devices are becoming a favourite are briefly discussed in Chapter 4.[41]

Tracing the Trail

Where are the militants in Jammu & Kashmir getting their weapons from? 'It is widely accepted by Western and non-Western experts that the ISI [Pakistani external intelligence agency] is the main body facilitating movement of weapons across the border to Kashmiri militants.'[42] In addition to the ISI, the militants also procure their weapons from the arms bazaars in the NWFP. The arms are routed through the western border of the state.

Predictably, the conflict, made violent through the availability of weapons, has brought about untold suffering and pain to the

[41] For a detailed analysis of the use of explosive devices by militants in South Asia, see Mallika Joseph and Suba Chandran, *Landmines and IEDs in South Asia*, New Delhi: Institute for Peace and Conflict Studies, 2001.

[42] Human Rights Watch, *India: Arms and Abuses in Indian Punjab and Kashmir*, vol. 6, no. 10, September 1994.

TABLE 2.2: WEAPONS RECOVERED FROM MILITANTS IN J&K

Type of Arms	1990	1991	1992	1993	1994	1995	1996	1997	1998	1999	2000	2001	2002	2003	Total
Assault rifles	1,240	2,320	3,504	2,209	2,196	2,055	2,150	1,725	1,520	1,244	1.405	1,646	1,571	1,440	26,621
Machine guns	77	151	165	154	152	76	102	81	81	59	51	43	22	40	1,267
Rocket launchers	173	112	159	78	115	80	91	119	244	186	112	192	108	119	1,937
Sniper rifles	–	–	9	54	41	38	49	60	34	13	16	12	7	11	350
Mortars	–	–	–	4	3	3	1	6	7	17	2	76	34	30	185
Pistols	751	849	756	921	940	965	1,052	1,024	584	385	482	370	308	344	9,841
Radio sets	–	–	29	132	211	246	413	444	583	409	460	462	503	664	4,757
Grenades	2,502	1,784	2,391	4,363	2,603	2,870	3,949	5,124	5,883	6,000	7,955	5,956	3,477	4,186	60,170
Ammunition (in millions)	0.188	0.272	0.321	0.313	0.456	0.343	0.356	0.294	0.321	0.220	0.309	2.941	0.147	0.159	6.710
Mines (APLM, AT)	750	136	226	592	1,006	634	552	408	541	305	386	264	111	163	6,085
Anti-aircraft guns	–	–	–	–	–	–	–	1	–	–	–	–	–	–	1
Missile launchers	–	–	–	–	–	–	–	1	1	2	—	1	–	–	5
Grenade throwers	–	–	–	–	–	–	–	–	21	6	52	–	–	7	86
Explosives (kg)	231	274	285	2,950	1,342	1,489	2,487	6,790	3,691	3,233	3,469	3,714	1,765	2,519	35,111

Source: http://www.armyinkashmir.org/weapons.html.

local population. Apart from the large-scale displacement of Kashmiri Pundits to Jammu and other parts of India, the conflict, particularly the kidnapping and killing of foreign tourists, has almost destroyed the tourist economy of the region. Most of the basic and developmental infrastructure has been destroyed, making the government's task all the more difficult in providing even some of the basic amenities to the people of the state. For example, the power situation is so severe that most homes and even police stations and offices have come to rely on inverters and generators for their power supply.

Humanitarian Fallout

Prolonged armed deployment in the conflict zone has not only resulted in battle fatigue but also a high incidence of human rights' violations. Responding to negative criticism, the armed forces have set in place mechanisms to check violations of human rights. But violations by terrorists continue unabated. This, to a large extent, is also tied to the increased presence of foreign terrorists in the conflict zone. Earlier, the militants were from the region itself, which deterred them from killing their own people. Now, however, the aim of the foreign terrorists is to create terror and anarchy, therefore, they do not despite to attack unarmed civilians. The statistics in Table 2.3 reveal the extent of the violence perpetrated in by the terrorists against civilians.

India's North-East

Another region beset by the problem of parallel insurgencies and armed conflict is India's north-east comprising the seven states of Assam, Manipur, Meghalaya, Arunachal Pradesh, Nagaland, Tripura, and Mizoram, which are linked tenuously to the rest of the country with only a 22-km. corridor connecting them to the mainland; 99 per cent of the borders are international and are shared with Bhutan, Bangladesh, China and Myanmar. These neighbours are not only home to several training camps of most of the insurgency groups operating in the region, but have also been their source of arms and ammunition. In November 2001,

TABLE 2.3: CIVILIANS KILLED BY TERRORISTS IN J&K

Type of Arms	1990	1991	1992	1993	1994	1995	1996	1997	1998	1999	2000	2001	2002	2003	2004*	Total
Civilians killed in terrorist firing	449	341	536	668	700	878	1,230	863	754	729	633	786	805	613	209	10,194
Civilians killed grenade attacks by militants in explosive/hand	12	41	98	79	120	153	106	85	103	92	129	133	117	112	68	1,448
Civilians injured in firing ex-plosions/hand grenades by militants	297	671	902	1,016	1,528	1,532	1,560	1,060	1,187	1,119	1,258	2,120	1,714	1,546	706	18,216
Abduction, including that of women by militants	169	290	281	349	368	548	666	448	298	241	286	335	318	319	90	5,006
Total civilian casualties by militants																
(a) Killed	461	382	634	747	820	1,031	1,336	938	867	821	762	919	922	725	277	11,642
(b) Injured	297	671	902	1,016	1,528	1,532	1,560	1,060	1,187	1,119	1,258	2,120	1,714	1,546	706	18,216
Civilians killed in crossfiring	539	524	435	310	249	171	88	82	110	116	180	179	128	111	35	3,257
Total civilian casualties	1,000	906	1,069	1,057	1,069	1,202	1,424	1,020	977	937	942	1,098	1,050	836	312	14,899

Note: * Till 31 May 2004.

Source: http://www.armyinkashmir.org/civilian.html.

the NA SA KA, the Myanmar special unit, arrested 36 insurgents from Manipur with 1,600 illegal weapons, all of Chinese origin. Earlier, in 1996, the Bangladesh security forces seized 500 AK-47 rifles, 80 machine guns, 50 rocket launchers and 2,000 grenades from two ships. Two Tamil (LTTE) rebels were also arrested in this regard. There is no dearth of statistics to reveal the level of arms availability in the neighbourhood on the one hand, and on the other, the vulnerability of the states that have a host of armed groups dipping their hands into the grey and black markets of the region.

There are at least 34 insurgent groups operating in Assam. Prominent among them are the United Liberation Front of Asom (ULFA), the National Democratic Front of Bodoland (NDFB), the Bodo Liberation Tigers (BLT), the United People's Democratic Solidarity (UPDS), Dima Halong Daoga (DHD), and the Muslim United Liberation Tigers of Asom (MULTA). The situation in the other states in the region is no better: Manipur has 35 militant groups, of which 18 are active; Tripura has about 19. Most of these militant groups have their bases in the neighbouring countries. Bhutan at one time had about 36 ULFA training camps. It is currently home to the headquarters of the ULFA and the NDFB. There are several training camps in Bangladesh as well.[43]

The various militant groups in the region, from the Naga National Council (NNC) onwards, have established and maintained links with similar movements in Myanmar, particularly the Kachins, who have provided militants with not only refugee and training camps, but also access to the black markets for small arms. Of all the subsequent guerrilla groups, the National Socialist Council of Nagaland (NSCN) has established itself as the prime group that in addition to being instrumental for the mushrooming of various insurgencies in the region, has also been their conduit for weapons for South-East Asia. This is because the NSCN controls the routes through which the arms enter the region.

With huge quantities of weapons entering the region, it has

[43] E.N. Rammohan, 'Manipur: Blueprint for Counter-Insurgency', *Faultlines*, vol. 12, May 2002, p. 21.

TABLE 2.4: ARMS RECOVERIES IN INDIA'S NORTH-EAST

	Tripura	Nagaland	Meghalaya	Manipur	Assam	Mizoram	Total
1991	85	3	0	22	212	0	322
1992	86	19	0	49	444	0	598
1993	59	16	5	164	226	0	470
1994	52	28	0	135	270	124	609
1995	251	95	1	154	95	65	661
1996	107	48	5	85	120	35	400
1997	95	50	14	211	124	4	498
1998	154	17	0	96	191	4	462
1999	76	16	22	67	168	5	354
2000	137	88	29	78	223	8	563
2001	95	107	18	74	287	32	613
2002*	61	130	49	75	229	15	559
Total	1,258	617	143	1,210	2,589	292	6,109

Note: *Data till 31 October.
Source: www.satp.org.

become a case of supply creating a demand. Discontented groups no longer exercise all available democratic means before resorting to armed violence.

Though it is impossible to determine the quantity of weapons with the militants, the statistics given in Table 2.4 are indicative of the quantity available.

It is believed that the ULFA has a stockpile of 5,000 weapons.[44] The stockpile with the NSCN is considered to be much larger though no figures are available.

Tracing the Trail

Most of the weapons coming into the north-east are from the black markets in Cambodia. Weapons are also procured from East European armies following the disintegration of the East Bloc. The trail of smuggled weapons begins from the Rangong Islands off the coast of Thailand. Through the Andaman Sea, the wea-

[44] Anindita Dasgupta, 'Small Arms Proliferation in North East: A Case Study of Assam', in Banerji, *South Asia at Gun Point*.

pons reach Cox Bazaar in Bangladesh, from where they are transported by various routes into India's north-east and Myanmar. Some of the weapons are transited north to the Chittagong Hills, and hence to the north-east through Mizoram, Tripura, or Assam. They also reach Nagaland through the North Cachar Hills and Karbi Anglong. Weapons also enter the north-east through the Arakans or through Sylhet. Once the weapons reach the north-east, they find their way to the various militant groups through thriving black markets in Dimapur (in Nagaland) and Shillong, the capital of Meghalaya state. The cost of the weapons appear rather steep, with an AK-47 costing Rs. 160,000 (US $3,800), an LMG Rs. 150,000 (US $3,700), a carbine Rs. 30,000 (US $700), and a 9 mm. pistol Rs. 30,000 (US $700).[45] The money for weapons is obtained primarily through extortion and kidnapping. The 600-plus tea gardens in Assam are the constant victims, coughing up huge amounts of money. The insurgent groups have also established a system of extorting money from the government agencies disbursing grants for various development activities.

Humanitarian Fallout

The humanitarian fallout has been, as usual, mass exodus and displacement: there are about 120,000 refugees belonging to the Santhal, Bengali Muslim, Rabha, and Hajong communities in about 100 relief camps in the Kokrajhar and Bongaigaon districts of Assam.[46] However, the basic generating infrastructure of the economy has not been totally destroyed, as in Kashmir, as this creates the base for the extensive extortion racket employed by the militants. Other developmental infrastructure has, of course, not been spared. Weapons have also sharpened traditional tribal and ethnic tensions, culminating in ethnic cleansing. Weapons in the hands of militants who have surrendered have emerged as another cause of serious concern, as these weapons are more often used as a means to successful criminal activity. While the conflict has driven away investors, and along with them employ-

[45] Ibid.

[46] Ibid.

ment opportunities, unemployment has risen sharply. This has, in turn, spawned discontent and provided an impetus for unemployed youth to join ranks of the insurgents.

Other Regions

Apart from the prime zones in Kashmir and the north-east, where incessant conflict continues, other states like Andhra Pradesh, Madhya Pradesh, Uttar Pradesh, Bihar, Jharkhand, Chhattisgarh, Maharashtra, Orissa, West Bengal and Tamil Nadu also exhibit unrest due to the presence of Naxalites—groups with extreme left orientation, who have no faith in the political system and wish to overthrow it. The two main Naxalite groups are the People's War Group (PWG) and the Maoist Communist Centre (MCC). These groups also have established linkages with the Maoists in Nepal.

The PWG, considered to be the most potent of the Naxalite groups, has about 1,100 full-time underground cadres and 5,000 overground sympathizers. It has in its possession a total of about 1,690 weapons, including 90 AK-47s, 650 revolvers and pistols, and 950 other weapons including double- and single-barrel guns.[47] The PWG specializes in using IEDs, mostly reported as landmine blasts in the media. The explosives primarily used are gelatin sticks, commonly used for blasting rocks in stone quarries.

Naxalites apart, caste armies and private militias, referred to as *senas*, are also found predominantly in the state of Bihar—about 12 such *senas* with various caste affiliations operate in Bihar. In addition to these, there is also a whole range of criminal gangs in most parts of India. All these smaller actors (Naxalites, *senas*, and criminal gangs), 'small' only in comparison to the militants in Kashmir and insurgents in the north-east, also use a variety of weapons, causing deaths of many civilians. The statistics in Tables 2.5 and 2.6 are indicative of the types of weapons in the possession of these groups.

[47] Ashok Das, 'Naxalism: Y2K Problem Sans Solution?', *Hindustan Times*, 7 January 2000.

TABLE 2.5: BREAK-UP OF FIREARMS RECOVERED FROM EXTREMIST GROUPS IN BIHAR

	Country-made	Regular	Total
1998	213	24	237
1999	197	39	236
2000	222	44	266
2001	231	50	281
2002*	134	53	187
Total	997	210	1,207

Note: Data till September 2002.

TABLE 2.6: EXPLOSIVES RECOVERED FROM EXTREMISTS IN BIHAR

Year	Country-made bombs	Regular grenades	Gelatin/ dynamite	Total
1998	29	5	285	319
1999	30	4	761	795
2000	38	4	146	188
2001	67	7	26	100
2002*	24	5	75	104
Total	188	25	1,293	1,506

Note: Data till September 2002.
Source: South Asia Terrorism Portal: www.satp.org.

THE CASE OF BANGLADESH

The situation prevailing in Bangladesh is somewhat unique when compared to other South Asian countries. There is no current armed conflict in any part of the country, but it is flooded with a whole range of weapons, and is the principal conduit for weapons entering India's north-east apart from housing a thriving black market into which most armed militant groups in the region dip their hands. The problem for Bangladesh arises due to the diffusion of these weapons into the society, thus contributing to an increase of gun culture in the country.

The principal users of small arms and light weapons are criminal gangs involved in a wide range of criminal activity, predominantly the smuggling of weapons. There are over 75 criminal gangs in Bangladesh, a third of which operate in the capital Dhaka alone. According to some estimates, Bangladesh has about 200,000 illicit weapons, a fourth of which are with the criminal gangs in Dhaka.[48]

Political parties are the next-largest users of small arms and light weapons. Most political parties have two fronts, one for political mobilization, and another (armed) for executing their coercive activities like silencing political opponents and indulging in contract grabbing. Aiding the politicians are also criminal gangs. It is estimated that four out of nine murders committed every day are with illicit weapons.[49] The political parties also indulge in an arms race amongst themselves, which has resulted in increased acquisitions of weapons by party members.

The rise in the use of weapons by university students is also a cause for concern, as this has led to an increase in violence on campuses. Students particularly have been involved in political activity, almost mirroring national politics within university campuses. All major political parties in Bangladesh have armed their student wings, thereby contributing to the increase in violence. Additionally, weapons are also available on hire from local criminal gangs during heightened campus activity which has violent undertones.

Apart from the spillover of arms that are in transit, Bangladesh is also plagued by the illegal production of a variety of weapons like 'pipe guns' and 'cut rifles'. Like the ones manufactured in India, these weapons are not of high quality. However, they serve the purpose of intimidation and extortion. The proliferation of small arms in Bangladesh has not led to a spiralling of ethnic discontent or conflict. However, it has led to the militarization of the society apart from increasing the use of weapons in political activity and permeating campus activity.

[48] Sohel Manzur, 'People's Security now the Biggest Challenge for Bangladesh', *Cyber Voice*, 2000: http://www.cybervoice-bd.net/lead.html.

[49] Ibid.

THE CASE OF NEPAL

In Nepal, traditionally, weapons were used for ceremonial purposes, at marriages or other such celebrations, besides being retained by the wealthy class as symbols of prestige and for hunting. This trend was further supplemented and enforced by a very stringent Arms Control Act, in place since 1962.[50] However, with the advent of the 1990s, there has been a marked difference in this trend. Two very important developments contributed to this; the introduction of multiparty democracy in place of absolute monarchy, and the rise of Maoist insurgency in 1996. Despite these developments, particularly the Maoist insurgency, the proliferation of small arms remains modest in Nepal when compared to its neighbours. The main reason has been a strict central government in the past, which was run by an absolute monarch. The exact number of firearms available is not clearly known. Though a vast number of Nepalis have served in the army as well as in the two world wars, and a considerable number of people are well versed in the use of firearms, guns have had restricted use.

The 1962 Arms and Ammunition Act has so far remained stringent in its stipulation on firearms. Individuals are not allowed to keep or obtain licences for handguns in their private capacity. The only guns that can be retained with a licence are 0.22 rifles and 12 bore guns, which fall mainly in the category of hunting weapons. According to the Act, it is illegal to hold, purchase, sell, modify or produce weapons that do not meet the licensing criteria laid down by the government.[51] Nepal does not have a significant domestic firearms industry and its single registered manufacturer of ammunition, Sundarial Military Factory, makes

[50] Williams James Arputharaj, Chamila Thushani Hemmathagama and Saradha Nanayakkara, *Small Arms Proliferation a Big Problem: A Study of Legislations in South Asia and the UN Programme of Action*, Colombo: South Asia Partnership International, 2003, p. 20.

[51] South Asia Partnership (SAP), *Canada, South Asia and Small Arms: Synthesis Report on National Consultation and Regional Strategy Meeting*, Ottawa: SAP Canada, 2002, pp. 18–22.

ammunition of more than 12.7 mm.[52] Nepal imports weapons from Germany, the UK, Belgium, Israel, and the US.[53]

The use of firearms varies in the two main geographical areas of the country—the mountains, and the Terai plains bordering India. The settlements in the mountainous area are centuries old, with a relatively homogeneous population. The Terai plains, on the other hand, are composed of a heterogeneous population still in the process of settling. Covered with thick forests till the recent past and bordering India, coupled with the open India–Nepal border, the Terai plains facilitate easy movement of criminal elements from both sides. Due to its proximity to the Indian states of Bihar and Uttar Pradesh, the effects of developments there are reflected in the Terai: the open display and brandishing of weapons by the major political parties in total disregard of the Arms Act serves as a means both for personal protection and for intimidating voters. Besides, with the criminalization of politics, criminal gangs active in border areas find patronage in both countries and render their services during elections on either side.[54]

Although organized crime is yet to take root in Nepal, the trafficking of contraband items as of well as arms and ammunition is becoming more open and frequent than in the past, and is on the rise due to urbanization, unemployment, and poverty. This has created a new demand for weapons of all kinds. From knives and the traditional *khukris*, the use and proliferation of firearms has become rampant.[55] After the restoration of democratic elections, there has been a marked tendency among politicians to arm themselves and use violence to win.

The rise of the Maoist insurgency has been coterminous with the return of multiparty democracy. At the launch of the 'people's war', the Maoists were equipped with nothing but a few guns

[52] Norwegian Initiative on Small Arms Transfers (NISAT), *Nepal Country Profile* (last updated 26 August 2003): http://www.nisat.org/nepal

[53] Ibid.

[54] Deepak Thapa and Amar Singh Shah, 'Small Arms and their Increasing Proliferation in Nepal', in Banerji, *South Asia at Gun Point*, pp. 97–8.

[55] Ibid., p. 99.

looted from local landlords, those acquired from local gunsmiths, and a very modest arsenal brought from India. However, over the years, their weaponry has improved greatly. Given the diverse sources of their supply, it is even believed that the Maoists have now acquired automatic weapons though they have not been used or recovered.

The various sources of weapons are:

1. Forcible collection of firearms belonging to the local population. In many cases people have brought their firearms to the police stations and district headquarters for safekeeping,
2. Ambushes or raids on police stations, weapons' depositories, and army stockpiles,[56]
3. Clandestine imports from illegal weapons production units in India—purchases in 2002 neared 2 billion Nepal rupees.[57]

Since the beginning of the insurgency, more than 7,000 people have died. According to government officials, Maoists control approximately 40 per cent of the territory.[58] The Maoists resort to robbing banks, looting ordinary people, and extortion to procure weapons from the illegal arms markets in India. The insurgents are also known to be increasingly using IEDs, which are more effective in terrorizing people. These Maoists have established and maintain links with left extremist groups like the MCC and PWG of India, which provide them with training besides weapons and material support.[59]

Soon after the Maoist uprising in the mid-1990s, the demand for weapons and licences increased manifold, especially in the Terai plains, and close to 11,000 arms were imported from countries other than India. In the beginning of January 2001, the government in a bid to check this practice announced a general amnesty, asking people to surrender their illegal weapons to the

[56] SAP, *Canada, South Asia and Small Arms*; also see Thapa and Shah, 'Small Arms and their Increasing Proliferation, p. 101.

[57] 'Flourishing Arms Trade', *Chennai Thanthi*, 30 December 2001, p. 28: http://www.nisat.org.

[58] SAP, *Canada, South Asia and Small Arms*, pp. 18–22.

[59] Thapa and Shah, 'Small Arms and their Increasing Proliferation', p. 102.

government, but this remained largely ineffective, as only a few people surrendered their weapons, with others giving or losing their weapons to the Maoists.[60] The current situation where Kathmandu is under virtual siege and held hostage by the Maoist forces, is indicative of a future trend which might lead to a further deterioration of law and order and spell more trouble for this mountainous state.

A tentative ceasefire was declared between the Nepal government and the Maoists in January 2003, to curb militancy and check the proliferation of small arms and light weapons in the country.[61] The government, after much debate, equipped the Royal Nepal Army with SLRs and provided training to fight the insurgents. Post-9/11, the Nepal government declared the Maoists as terrorists and succeeded in getting substantial military assistance from the US. The government has recently brokered a deal with Colt Manufacturing of the US for 50,000–60,000 M16 rifles, and with FN Herstal of Belgium for 5,500 light machine guns. The US partially funded the rifle purchase with an assistance package of $12 million. Arms transfers began in January 2003 and are expected to continue over the next few years.[62]

[60] Ibid., p. 20.

[61] SAP International, *Comparative Study of Small Arms Legislation in Bangladesh, India, Nepai, Pakistan and Sri Lanka*, Kathmandu: SAP International, 2003, pp. 36–7.

[62] GIIS, *Small Arms Survey 2003: Development Denied*, Oxford: Oxford University Press, 2003, p. 113.

CHAPTER 3

International Efforts: Best Practices

Over the last decade, much regional and international action has come about to tackle the proliferation of small arms and light weapons. This chapter attempts to discuss a few of these initiatives that could help South Asia in absorbing these as best practices. The initiatives examined here are those that have established a trend in regional and global cooperation.

REGIONAL INITIATIVES

It is generally believed that regional measures are more effective than global efforts towards controlling the spread of small arms.[1] The European Union's Council of Ministers adopted an eight-point set of guidelines that needs to be followed prior to a transfer of arms. One of the salient features of the guidelines is analysis of the domestic situation in the recipient country prior to the transfer of weapons. The analysis is to include the destination country's commitment to human rights, the ongoing conflict within the recipient country or its vicinity, etc. Following this, in 1997, the EU established a programme to prevent and combat the transfer of illicit weapons. This was followed by the adoption of a Code of Conduct in 1998, aimed at regulating the transfer of weapons.

The Organization of American States (OAS) too has worked towards curbing the proliferation of small arms. Initiated by Colombia and Mexico, the problem of the illicit trafficking of weapons was linked to the narcotics trade, and the OAS was successful in signing the Inter-American Convention Against

[1] International Committee of the Red Cross, *Arms Availability and the Situation of Civilians in Armed Conflict*, Geneva: ICRC, 1999.

the Illicit Manufacturing of and Trafficking in Firearms, Ammunition, Explosives and Other Related Materials in November 1997.

The west African states have also been active in promoting a moratorium on the production and import of weapons among them. Their action has encouraged other regional organizations to initiate similar measures against small arms proliferation. The Southern Africa Development Community also came up with its Southern Africa Regional Action Plan which aimed at arresting illicit arms transfers, destruction of surplus weapons, and a call for increased transparency in national measures against the illicit transfer of weapons.

GLOBAL INITIATIVES

The UN was the first body to address the issue of arms trade. However, it has failed to be consistent in its efforts. Nevertheless, in the last few years it has displayed renewed commitment to the cause of stemming small arms proliferation in a comprehensive manner. It's POA, following the 2001 UN Conference on the Illicit Trade in Small Arms and Light Weapons in All Its Aspects, has met with reasonable success and is discussed in the following section. Other global initiatives that have contributed towards raising awareness and called for concerted action against the proliferation of small arms include the Brussels Call For Action which was aimed particularly at post-conflict reconstruction with specific emphasis on disarming former combatants, the initiatives by the Group of Like-Minded States, the Group of Eight (G-8), and the initiative by Nobel laureates.

Notwithstanding all these measures, a remarkable development in the discourse of small arms has been the involvement of the global civil society. Its participation and successful action was established through the global campaign against landmines, which not only succeeded in bringing to world attention the need to ban landmines, but also in coercing state parties to drastically reduce the use of weapons and invest time and resources in mine action. The same trend, though to a lesser degree, is apparent in the debate on small arms. Advocacy on small arms has not been as intense as that on landmines, primarily because the small arms campaign aims not at banning the use of weapons, but only in regulating their use, trade and transfer.

PROGRAMME OF ACTION

The 2001 UN conference on Illicit Trade in Arms and Light Weapons in All Its Aspects resulted in the adoption of the POA. Since then, the POA, adopted by consensus, has been successful in serving as the minimum guidelines that member states follow with regard to stemming the proliferation of small arms and light weapons. The minimum standards set by the POA have brought to light a large volume of hitherto unknown literature on state activity (in some cases) and inactivity (in some others), relating to curbing and controlling the spread of small arms. Table 3.1 details national implementation of the POA with regard to the South Asian states.

India, Pakistan, and Sri Lanka have set up a national coordination agency to supervise and implement the framework laid out by the POA. With the exception of Bangladesh, the other countries have made legislation regarding all four facets of production, import, export and transit. Bangladesh has yet to make legislation on the transit of weapons through its territory. India is the only country in the region to have a national system for the export and import of weapons, whereas Pakistan has a national system for control over arms brokering. With regard to manufacture and possession, all four countries have domestic legislation supervising these aspects, but only India and Pakistan cover stockpiling and trade which are also covered in the domestic legislation of all the regional countries except Sri Lanka. The Sri Lankan government is now also considering the expansion of domestic legislation to bring into its net effective stockpile management. Similarly, there is varied response from the regional countries with regard to other aspects of the issue, such as Pakistan carrying out a de-weaponization campaign and the destruction of surplus weapons after a review of existing stocks, whereas India already has a reintegration programme in place.

TABLE 3.1: NATIONAL IMPLEMENTATION OF POA BY SOUTH ASIAN COUNTRIES

States/ Period	Bangladesh	India	Nepal	Pakistan	Sri Lanka
National					
National Coordination Agency	–	✓	–	✓	✓
National Point of Contact	✓	✓	–	✓	✓
Laws and Procedures on:					
Production	✓	✓	✓	✓	✓
Export	✓	✓	✓	✓	✓
Import	✓	✓	✓	✓	✓
Transit	–	✓	✓	✓	✓
National System of Export and Import					
Licensing or Authorization					
Diversion Risk	–	✓	–	–	–
End-user Certificates	–	✓	–	–	–
Retransfers	–	–	–	–	–
Brokering Controls	–	–	–	✓	–
Domestic Legislation					
Manufacture	✓	✓	✓	✓	✓
Possession	✓	✓	✓	✓	✓
Stockpiling	–	✓	–	✓	–
Trade	✓	✓	✓	✓	–
Stockpile Management	–	–	–	–	Under consideration
Review of Procedures	–	✓	–	–	–
Regular Reviews of Stocks	–	✓	–	✓	–
Surplus	–	–	–	–	✓
Collected	–	–	–	✓	–
Policy of Destroying All	–	–	–	–	–
Disarmament and Weapons Collection	✓	–	–	–	–
Disarmament, Demobilization, Reintegration	–	–	–	–	✓
Other	–	✓	–	De-weaponization amnesty	–
Financial or Technical Assistance	–	–	–	–	Receives aid

Source: IANSA, 'National Implementation in Asia', London: IANSA, *Implementing the Programme of Action 2003*, pp. 114–15.

Though individual countries have undertaken measures for the successful implementation of the POA, as the following narrative on India and Pakistan indicates,[2] the region still lacks a concerted effort under the aegis of SAARC or other organization. According to the *Implementing the Programme of Action 2003* by IANSA, there have been efforts to engage the regional actors, but without much success.[3] However, there is overwhelming support from the regional countries towards cooperating at the regional level.[4]

INDIA AND THE POA

India has designated its Joint Secretary, Disarmament and International Security Affairs Division, Ministry of External Affairs, as the national point of contact for matters relating to the implementation of the POA. It also set up an Inter-Ministerial Task Force in 2002 to provide policy guidance and research, apart from monitoring the country's activities relating to small arms.[5]

The Arms Act (1959) and the Arms Rules (1962) contain com-

[2] Apart from India and Pakistan, Sri Lanka and Bangladesh have also submitted their national implementation reports. While the Bangladesh report is too brief to quote, the Sri Lanka report is rather substantial in detailing various measures undertaken to implement the POA. However, a narrative based on the Sri Lanka report has not been included for want of space. The entire report is accessible at: http://disarmament.un.org:8080/cab/docs/nationalreports/2002/sri-lanka.pdf. The other reports are also accessible online.
India: http://disarmament.un.org:8080/cab/docs/nationalreports/2002/ndia.pdf; Pakistan: http://disarmament.un.org:8080/cab/docs/nationalreports/2002/Pakistan.pdf; and Bangladesh: http://disarmament.un.org:8080/cab/docs/nationalreports/2002/bangladesh.pdf

[3] Bangladesh, with the backing of the Canadian and UK governments, had made several vain attempts in 2002 at getting the South Asian countries together.

[4] The national implementation reports of the countries in South Asia indicate their favourable disposition towards regional cooperation on this issue.

[5] Based on the Report on National Implementation by the Government of India, 'Implementation of the United Nations Programme of Action to Prevent, Combat and Eradicate the Illicit Trade in Small Arms and Light Weapons in All Its Aspects', 2003.

prehensive legal requirements relating to the manufacture, sale, transfer, transport, export and import of arms and ammunition, and penal provisions for violations of these. These are supplemented by other laws like the Prevention of Terrorism Act, the Armed Forces (Special Powers) Act, the Indian Penal Code, and the Army Act.

The government controls the manufacture of revolvers, pistols and rifled weapons, and production is disallowed in the private sector despite the liberalization of the economy and a licensing regime for major industries.

The weapons manufactured in India are uniquely marked and, according to the Arms Act (1959), weapons with no identification marks cannot be sold or transferred, and any person in possession of any weapon with no identification marks is presumed to have removed/obliterated the marks unless proven otherwise.

Following an increase in armed terrorist activity in the late 1980s, the government has substantially withdrawn the licence-issuing powers of the state/district authorities: proper licences are required for the possession of a weapon. Even the licence issued is restricted to particular geographical areas.

PAKISTAN AND THE POA

According to the Report on the National Implementation of the POA submitted in July 2003, Pakistan has established a national point of contact for concerted and coordinated effort in the country with regard to the implementation of the POA; the Director General of the United Nations and Disarmament Division of the Ministry of Interior has been set up as the coordinating agency. Additionally, for the last few years, a special cell has been in existence in the Ministry of Interior, which deals exclusively with the fallout of linkages between organized crime, terrorist networks, and illicit small arms and light weapons.[6]

[6] Based on the Report on National Implementation by the Islamic Republic of Pakistan, 'Implementation of the United Nations Programme of Action to Prevent, Combat and Eradicate the Illicit Trade in Small Arms and Light Weapons in All Its Aspects', 2003.

The Arms Act of 1878, the Pakistan Arms Ordinance of 1965, the Surrender of Illicit Arms Act of 1991 are some of the items of legislation in place that regulate the production, import, export, transit, transfer, retransfer, and possession of small arms and light weapons. Pakistan is engaged in a multi-pronged strategy to remove weapons from its society, as it views the proliferation of weapons within the context of organized crime, drug trafficking, money laundering, and terrorist activities.

The government initiated a phased de-weaponization programme in 2001 which resulted in the recovery/confiscation of 250,000 weapons until April 2003. Barring those weapons that could be put to reuse subject to laid-out procedures, the rest were destroyed. Pakistan is positively disposed towards regional and international cooperative arrangements aimed at controlling the spread of illegal weapons.

BEYOND THE POA

Despite the successful implementation of the POA, comprehensive control of small arms proliferation is a long way off. This is because a few pertinent issues which were debated at length could not be included in the POA for want of consensus. Two of the most prominent ones that were not included were: (i) arms brokering, and (ii) the marking and tracing of weapons. Nevertheless, some progress has been made towards addressing these two concerns. A third issue which is yet to receive due attention is the need for adequate restrictions on the sale or banning the sale of small arms and light weapons to NSAs.

The Secretary General of the UN constituted a Group of Governmental Experts to study the feasibility of an international instrument to identify and trace illicit small arms and light weapons. Subsequent to the group's recommendation, an Open-Ended Working Group has been constituted to Negotiate an Inter-national Instrument to Enable States to identify and trace, in a Timely and Reliable Manner, Illicit Small Arms and Light

Weapons. The Group had its first meeting on 16 June 2004.[7]

Similarly, with regard to brokerage, informal consultations have commenced for discussing steps to enhance international co-operation in preventing, combating, and eradicating illicit brokering. The third round of these informal consultations was held on 11 June 2004, and one of the recommendations that emerged towards the end of the informal consultations was to establish a Group or Panel of Government Experts, like the one set up to discuss tracing and marking of small arms.[8]

Marking and tracing of weapons, in addition to greater transparency in arms brokerage, has been a concern predominantly expressed by the developed countries which are the principal weapons producers.[9]

[7] Statement by Jayant Prasad, Ambassador and Permanent Representative of India to the Conference on Disarmament, Geneva, at the Open-Ended Working Group to Negotiate an International Instrument to Enable States to Identify and Trace, in a Timely and Reliable Manner, Illicit Small Arms and Light Weapons.

[8] Summary of the broad-based consultations on further steps to enhance international cooperation in preventing, combating and eradicating illicit brokering in small arms and light weapons, United Nations Headquarters, New York, 11 June 2004.

[9] Virginia Gamba, 'Arms Control and Disarmament: What Can the UN do to Strengthen its Work in the Area of Small Arms and Conventional Weapons Control?', accessed on 12 June 2004: http://www.unglobalsecurity.org/pdf/gamba.pdf

CHAPTER 4

Unexplored Dimensions: Explosive Devices and Illegal Production

Two issues that have remained outside the scope of the POA, or for that matter any concerted effort against the proliferation of small arms, have been the use of explosive devices and illegal domestic production. This chapter makes a modest attempt at highlighting the damage these two can cause, and argues for the need to have an inclusive debate.

IMPROVISED EXPLOSIVE DEVICES

The mandate of the POA has rightly been restricted so as to enable the widest cooperation possible. However, with increased cooperation, it should not be impossible to include issues that were earlier not debated at length for want of consensus. One of the issues that warrants inclusion is explosives. India has been highlighting this even during its participation in the earlier conference leading to the formalization of the POA; it has consistently requested for adequate attention on small arms as well as explosives. India's concern is valid considering the increase in the use of explosives by terrorists on its soil. However, these concerns are unlikely to remain peculiar to India alone. With restrictions on illicit trade on small arms bound to increase, and the easy availability of weapons becoming a challenge, militant groups are more likely to switch over to the use of explosive devices rather than continue their reliance on small arms. This trend,[1] clearly visible

[1] A comparative analysis of statistics on weapons and explosives seized in Jammu & Kashmir indicates that there is a substantive reduction in the number of weapons seized over the years. However, in the case of explosives, from 18 IEDs in 1991, the number rose to 718 in 2000, and from no seizures of RDX until 1995, the number has risen to 1,662 kg. in 2001.

in the conflict zones in India, is in all probability likely to be emulated in other zones as well, the spate of bombings and ambushes in Iraq and Pakistan being an indicator.

IEDs could become the prime tool of terror for all entities fighting against the state for the following reasons.

IEDs are Easy to Make

Apart from the explosive, the other ingredients required to make a simple but potent IED can be obtained from any marketplace. An IED is basically an explosive packed in a container with a fuse and shrapnel. The fuse is attached to a trigger mechanism, which can range from simple battery-operated ones to complex ones containing a remote control or timer pencils. There is no single way to make an IED, and the ingenuity of the IED is constrained only by the ingenuity of the human mind. The production of simple IEDs requires no expert knowledge, though complex IEDs require training and expertise. The explosive is the important part of the IED. Both gelatin sticks and plastic explosives have been used in India.

IEDs are Potent

All IEDs are potentially lethal regardless of the type of explosive used. The only determining factor is the quantity used. While large quantities of gelatin are requied to produce the desired effect, only a portion of that quantity of plastic explosives is required to produce the same effect. Only 700 gm. of RDX was used by the LTTE human bomb Dhanu to assassinate Rajiv Gandhi and 16 others. Contrast this with the 33,949 kg. of plastic explosives recovered from Kashmiri militants alone: it is not hard to imagine the catastrophe these explosives would have caused.

IEDs are Easy to Hide/Hard to Detect

In its unassembled form, it is virtually impossible to detect an IED. With two to three people carrying the different components of IEDs, it is feasible for them to slip through despite the most stringent security measures in place. Juxtapose this with any small arm or light weapon, which runs the risk of detection in any search operation.

IEDs can be Camouflaged

Most often, IEDs are packaged in common household objects like gas cylinders, pressure cookers, and milk cans, or steel pipes and fire extinguishers. The choice of a heavy metal container only adds to the lethality of the blast.

IEDs are Demoralizing

Because it is easy to camouflage these weapons, the psychological effect obtained is devastating. Forces in conflict-prone zones are much more fearful of IEDs than of encounters or direct firing.

IEDs are Target- and Time-Specific

Target- and time-specificity are the operational advantages of this weapon. IEDs are target-specific in the sense that they can be triggered at exactly the moment the target approaches, which in most instances is the security convoy. Hundreds of vehicles might pass by unharmed until the security convoy is targeted. Target-specificity enables insurgents to choose the targets, and it minimizes collateral damage which might impinge on their popular support base. Groups aiming to terrorize have resorted to using IEDs against civilians, specifically in crowded places like markets and bus terminals. An innocuous looking object is designed to explode only at a specific time, when the damage would be the maximum.

IEDs are Militant-Friendly

This is one of the greatest advantages accruing to militants in combat. In any encounter/ambush, the militants cannot rule out casualties on their side. The success rate of the operation might be further hampered if the attack is challenged by the security forces (targets). The IED, on the other hand, can kill an entire security convoy and inflict untold material damage, with no casualties whatsoever to the militants. It offers the militants crucial operational space to maximize target casualty and minimize losses to themselves.

ILLEGAL DOMESTIC PRODUCTION OF SMALL ARMS

Another area on which not much international attention has been focused remains illegal domestic production. The logic is that the global black market is awash with weapons that will take ages to deplete. If the regular supply of small arms in the clandestine market becomes more difficult with the concerted global action on illegal transit and transfer but situations that give birth to insurgencies and the demand for small arms have not been addressed, where will the terrorists turn to for weapons? They would either change their tactics and find an alternative to small arms or they would produce their own weapons.

Another argument has been that country-made weapons are not half as lethal as their factory-made counterparts. According to available statistics, there were 836 casualties in 2003[2] due to armed violence in Jammu & Kashmir. In comparison, in (Bihar and Uttar Pradesh, where more criminal rather than terrorist activity takes place), about more than 4,000 firearms-related mortalities occur every year.[3] This proves that use-and-throw country-made weapons are not any the less lethal, though they might be found wanting in automatic and sophisticated firepower. Therefore, illegal domestic production certainly deserves more attention than it currently receives.

THE CASE OF INDIA

In India, a number of illegal production units exist in Bihar, especially central Bihar, where hundreds of villages are involved in illegal gun manufacture. Bihar apart, illegal manufacturing of weapons is rampant in Uttar Pradesh and to some extent in Gujarat,

[2] http://www.armyinkashmir.org/civilian.html (till 31 May 2004).
[3] National Crime Records Bureau, *Crime in India 2002*, New Delhi, 2003.

West Bengal, Andhra Pradesh, and Punjab.[4] The supply to Delhi's criminal gangs comes from Gujarat, Jammu & Kashmir, and particularly Meerut district in Uttar Pradesh. There are anywhere from 500 to 650 illegal manufacturing units in Uttar Pradesh. The number varies because the units are such that they can easily commence, increase, reduce, cease, or resume manufacture of illegal small arms.

Referred to as *kattas*, the pistols are manufactured in innocuous-looking cycle/motorcycle/water pump/motor repair shops using plumbing pipes, bicycle frames, or any hollow steel pipe; other requirements like springs, wooden butts, triggers and hammers for releasing bullets are also easily available. On the lighter side, it has been remarked that most trains plying in Bihar have no passenger support columns, because all these pipes have been looted for the manufacture of guns!

The best *kattas* are available from the Rampur and Moradabad districts (western UP), parts of eastern UP like Deoria, Azamgarh, and Varanasi districts, and parts of western and central Bihar like Madhubani, Jehanabad, and Bhagalpur districts. The greatest availability is on the state's border with Nepal, declining towards the Madhya Pradesh and Jharkhand regions.

A country-made weapon can be obtained for as little as Rs. 300 ($6) if obtained directly from the manufacturer, and could go up to Rs. 1,000 ($20) if passing through multiple intermediaries. However, prices tend to fluctuate prior to local self-governing body elections; after the formation of coalition governments; following droughts, famines, bad monsoons, sudden food shortages on account of inflation or disruption of the PDS; or following a hike in fuel prices.

Though their accuracy is very low, *kattas* are very good at point-blank range. Usually having a single chamber, they can fire either 0.315 or 0.303 rounds. Despite being popular among organized criminals/mafia and first-time petty criminals, the weapon has

[4] The entire section on illegal domestic production is based on interviews conducted by Mallika Joseph with media and police personnel in Uttar Pradesh in April–May 2004.

inherent disadvantages. Most of them are mono-chamber handguns: those with multiple chambers are prone to jamming and misfiring because of the tremendous heat generated during firing. Also, there is no automatic firing capacity. Being heavy, long and cumbersome, they tend to produce a loud sound every time a round is fired, and require a long cooling period before they can be used again.

However, their unique criminal-friendly advantages easily score over the disadvantages. First, they are economical and there is no handgun in the world that is cheaper than the *katta*. It is literally a use-and-throw weapon which meets the illegal requirements of criminals. Being easily available and requiring no licensing, simply because its presence is not acknowledged, it is very effective, as non-recovery by law enforcement agencies means that the killers/criminals would be discharged/acquitted for the crimes for which they have been 'charge-sheeted'. The pins used in *kattas* generally do not leave the kind of typical distinctive marks as the factory-made ones do. Hence even the authentic recovery of a weapon by law enforcement agencies may not enable them to get foolproof evidence against the offenders. This also helps in concealing the point of manufacture, making tracing virtually impossible.

In 2002, about 4,098 people were killed by firearms in Uttar Pradesh; in Bihar, the number of casualties was 1,413.[5] Although it is true that guns don't kill people and only people kill people, it is more true to say that more people with guns can kill more people than more people without guns can kill people.

Where do the law enforcement agencies stand in this? They are part of the clientele that the illegal manufacturing units serve. Most often, armed only with wooden batons but directed to pursue criminals equipped with firepower, several policemen like beat constables procure these weapons for their own safety: the 'ultimate poor man's gun comes in handy for the poor police constable'. Second, with the proliferation of the encounter cul-

[5] National Crime Records Bureau, *Crime in India 2002*, New Delhi, 2003, Table 3.7.

ture, the police kill gangsters or other suspects and plant *kattas* on them to show that there was an exchange of fire prior to the encounter.

As of now, these illegal manufacturing units cater only to the small-time criminal and caste armies. Most of the NSAs and high-profile criminal and mafia gangs have access to the grey and black markets and the means to procure sophisticated weaponry. With regular international sources drying up, NSAs and criminal gangs are likely to seek their supply from illegal domestic production, and to that extent they would be prepared to make the requisite investments to upgrade the quality of these weapons to international standards.

The Case of Pakistan

The main focus with respect to illegal weapons proliferation in Pakistan remains on the unorganized private enterprise at Darra and Landi Kotal, where the arms trade continues without any state hindrance. In comparison, the POF, as mentioned earlier, makes mainly military-specific ammunition, whose production cost is relatively high. Second, POF-manufactured ammunition has a very limited and restricted clientele. Another contributing factor for the prolferation of illegal aims is that the POF sells only through designated distributors.

Besides this, the organized sector manufacturers are also bound to sell their products to licenced buyers only, which again limits their sale capacity. The overall number of licenced gun owners is not more than approximately 80,000–90,000 in the country. This makes the legal market a very small one, which is adequately served by the private producers.[6]

However, recent trends indicate that the estimated number of weapons in circulation is much higher than tabulated. The rising ethno-sectarian strife, civil war in Afghanistan, and an enhanced sense of insecurity arising out of factors such as poor economic conditions, bad governance and the deteriorating law-and-order

[6] Agha, 'Light Weapons Manufacture', in *Project on Light Weapons*, BASIC Working Paper No. 2, p. 5.

situation have raised the level of frustration and discontent. It is witnessed that the rising sense of apathy and social injustice has strengthened the appeal of small arms and light weapons. Darra and its cheaper rates attracts not only NSAs who purchase these weapons in bulk, but also a second category of buyers, such as officials, law-enforcing agents, influential politicians, and feudal and tribal lords who regard the possession of light weapons as a status symbol. Moreover, the various governments too have exacerbated this situation by giving licences for prohibited bore weapons to politicians and influential people to win political favour, or in pursuit of their vested interests in arming one (ethnic/sectarian) group against another from time to time.

The principal source of weapons proliferation and supply to areas of regional and domestic conflict, the unorganized sector, has a minimal manufacturing capacity of a hundred weapons per day.[7] With the very sudden and dramatic termination of the Afghan conflict, the governments following Zia's proved to be ineffective in solving this menace. Although attempts were made in the past, and are being made presently, too, to curb both the proliferation and the indiscriminate use of small arms, they are very much an indicator of a dysfunctional State apparatus.

In Pakistan, the failure of governance—especially with regard to narcotics production and smuggling—and the country's proximity to Afghanistan and its involvement in the attempts to end Soviet occupation of the country have combined to intensify an already dire law-and-order situation. In many cases, access to light weapons has facilitated or intensified conflicts, often by emboldening the protagonists. Consequently, the ability of the security forces has declined, corresponding to the increased firepower enjoyed by the forces pitched against them.

Second in line are the private manufacturers who operate and produce certain non-prohibited bore weapons under licence. Organized legal arms manufacturers are limited in number, and are concentrated mainly in the province of Punjab and in Karachi. Although the licensing requirements restrict the manufacturers

[7] Ibid.

from producing anything other than the exact configurations of the armaments, the main incentive or motivation for private enterprises is to generate profit, a task that becomes increasingly difficult in the restricted business environment as mentioned earlier, whereas on the one hand, these gun manufacturers are constrained by licence regulations, and on the other, they are provided with no incentives and are also heavily taxed by the government.

These private entrepreneurs are forced to continue with the production of the same items, whether or not they have any market demand, because of the licensing requirements. This proves to be an extremely cost-intensive effort, and in a bid to cover production costs as well as maintain a reasonable profit level, these manufacturers not only use substandard material, but are also involved in unauthorized manufacturing, their main business interests being in Darra. Accordingly, in many cities there are few or no licenced manufacturers, but many dealerships and repair licence holders are to be found. The end-users in this regard are usually NSAs or outfits that purchase these items for coercive activities.[8]

With respect to the scope of the term 'illicit trade', one should consider the illicit manufacture, acquisition, possession, use, and storage of small arms and light weapons, since these are closely linked to transfers of such weapons. The illicit trade in small arms and light weapons is closely related to the excessive and destabilizing accumulation and transfer of such arms, and should, therefore, not be limited to criminal breaches of existing arms legislation and export/import controls, but consideration should be given to all relevant factors.[9]

However, the illicit gunsmiths of India are poor cousins when compared to those of DAK. Darra is the heart of Pakistan's notorious arms bazaar, and it is here that one can acquire practically any small arm at a low cost: Kalashnikovs, M-16s, Uzis, and even

[8] Ibid.

[9] The 1999 Report of the UN Group of Governmental Experts on Small Arms, August 1999.

guns hidden in walking sticks and ballpoint pens. Some are originals left over from the war in Afghanistan, others are copies made in back-alley workshops, repaired originals, or copies made from cannibalized parts. Often the only difference between the original and the local designs is that locally manufactured barrels are made from inferior quality metal. Original AK-47s sell for about US $320, but an identical copy starts at US $50.

The Darra gunsmiths are famous for their skills and expertise, which have been passed down from father to son for generations, and they are known for their ability to produce any kind of weapon in spartan conditions. Although these artisans do not have any formal technical training, they have inherited the skills and have the ability to copy and make almost any kind of light weapon. Before the Soviet invasion of Afghanistan in December 1979, they produced mainly rifles and shotguns in addition to a wide range of pistols. Now they are adept at producing exact copies of any light weapon desired in a matter of days. They have been known to make imitation Chinese laser-sight pistols and Japanese pen pistols down to the finest detail.[10] Some of Darra's older craftsmen have also invented their own designs; for example a shotgun that works like a revolver, with a chamber holding six shells.[11] Unlike the previous two categories of gun manufacturers, the Darra gunsmiths base their business on demand and supply and are acutely aware of the prevalent market trends and demand factors.

At one time they supplied the Afghan *mujahideen* in their struggle against Soviet occupation. Now they are the main suppliers of guns to Kashmir and to Pakistan's troubled provinces of Punjab and Sind. Darra's shops and factories offer home delivery anywhere in the country, and are known to have also sold arms to guerrillas from Northern Ireland and the Middle East.[12]

As mentioned above, the arms bazaars of DAK and Landi Kotal in the NWFP have been famous for the production of light wea-

[10] Tara Kartha, 'South Asia: A Rising Spiral of Proliferation', *Background Paper*, Geneva: Small Arms Survey, 2000.

[11] Kevin Sullivan, 'Kalashnikovs at the Corner', *Nation*, 2 August 1998.

[12] Ibid.

pons for centuries. Both a colonial as well as a Cold War legacy, these traditional grey areas gained increased salience after the Soviet invasion of Afghanistan. This brought a new dimension to light weapons manufacture and production in this area—the unabated and immeasurable proliferation and inflow of illicit and illegal arms. Before the Soviet incursion, Darra used to produce mainly 9 mm. rifles, shotguns and pistols ranging from 0.22 to 0.32 calibre, etc. The Darra manufacturers are now adept at producing very exact copies of Kalashnikovs, bazookas, and even rocket launchers.

With regard to the illegal and illicit trade and manufacture and leakage points, this industry and the surrounding tribal belt is of most relevance.

An important characteristic of Darra and its various manufacturing units is that it is an unorganized enterprise, free from any state licensing, regulation and tax requirements. It is a part of the NWFP's tribal belt where no formal state law has been accepted or applied, and the tribal authority, better known as the *Jirga*, mediates and enforces justice, law and order. The government also cannot do much about the production/sale of weapons here, because the state laws do not have jurisdiction over the Tribal Areas—even the British couldn't establish their writ here. The government can only check the in-country movement of arms from this area, which is indeed a very challenging task.

Arms purchasers are attracted to the Darra because the manufacturing cost of weapons made here is relatively low compared to the state-regulated gunmaking sectors and the ready availability of a wide variety of weapons with so much pilferage taking place across the border. As mentioned earlier, the Darra is free from state regulations and restrictions plus the major source of raw material is available locally. The main features of the weapons made at Darra whether *locally* or through *conversion* (i.e. putting together foreign-made components taken from different weapons) are they are low in cost and thus do not have a high markup; and there is still scope for better quality control.

These arms bazaars of Pakistan are perhaps the best-known example of small-scale production of small arms. Hundreds of one-room operations manufacture copies of AK-47s and other rifles and pistols. Individual craftsmen manufacture small numbers of weapons, with a pistol taking three days to produce and an AK-47 between seven and ten days. But because there are many hundreds of such arms sellers, the overall production figures run into thousands of weapons.[13]

Most home-made production of small arms is unauthorized, if not illegal, from the point of view of the state in which it occurs. In some cases, however, the state itself engages in unauthorized small arms production by reverse engineering another country's or company's product, or by exceeding its permissible licenced production quota. Such production is illicit in that the owner of the original product has not given permission for production, but the manufacture of such weapons is often undertaken by state-owned companies or by private companies that are authorized by state agencies.

[13] 'Gun Dealers Fight for Trade', *BBC News*, 27 January 2000. Also see Pete Abel, 'Manufacturing Trends: Globalising the Source', in Lumpe, *Small Arms Control: Old Weapons*, New Issues, Chap. 4, pp. 85–7.

CHAPTER 5

National and Regional Initiatives

DE-WEAPONIZATION IN PAKISTAN

In response to the rising social violence and the easy availability of automatic weapons, in the autumn of 2000, the Pakistani government initiated a national arms control campaign. The main goal of the campaign was to facilitate de-weaponization through the confiscation and prosecution of illegally held arms. Initially, owners were encouraged to register licenced weapons. During the second stage, owners could surrender illegal firearms over a two-week amnesty in June 2001. Although the number of weapons received was not expected to be great, the hope was that these measures would break the culture of freely carrying Kalashnikov rifles in public and facilitate future police intervention.[1] According to the 1998 census, Pakistanis owned around 2 million licenced firearms. In addition, officials of the Ministry of Interior believe that there are roughly 18 million more held illegally. While there is no reason to doubt the scale of these numbers, they may give a misleading impression of the distribution of small arms in Pakistani society. Much like their counterparts in the US and other countries, Pakistani firearm owners typically have more than one gun. Till recently, firearm ownership was concentrated in a section of the population, such as the NWFP and Baluchistan more than in Sind and Punjab, a trend that is now rapidly changing. Out of a total population of some 140 million, firearms' ownership appears to extend to some 4–6 million individuals. Compared with the 20 million firearms in public hands, the inventories of the Armed Forces appear to be much smaller. The Pakistan Armed

[1] GIIS, 'Red Flags and Buicks: Global Firearm Stockpiles', *The Small Arms Survey: Counting the Human Cost*, Oxford: Oxford University Press, 2002, p. 99.

Forces, with a total active and reserve strength of 1.3 million, probably have at least 3 million small arms of all types.

This arms recovery and de-weaponization campaign was unique in the sense that, compared to earlier arms recovery efforts worldwide, it was launched by the government and was very well organized. Campaigns elsewhere, such as in Australia, the Balkans, Brazil, Northern Ireland, Latin America (El Salvador, Guatemala, Panama), Scotland, Africa (Mali, Mozambique, Niger, Sierra Leone, and South Africa) have usually been carried out by the non-governmental sector, community development organizations, UN peacekeepers, or were merely regional initiatives.

In May 2001, the Cabinet approved a New Arms Control Policy and Action Plan for the Recovery of Illicit Weapons. A ban had been imposed on the display of weapons throughout the country in February 2000, while the issue of fresh arms licences was stopped totally from March 2000.

The following weaknesses were noticed during the campaign.

1. The trend in recovery was slow and unsatisfactory during the post-amnesty phase, casting shadows on the resolve of the government and the fate of the campaign.
2. A total of 10,187 cases had been registered during the post-amnesty phase (till August 2001), but regrettably, to date, there have been no convictions.
3. So far, 9,663 persons have been arrested of whom 1,182 have been *challaned* (fined). In other words, this means that 8,481 persons are awaiting either investigation or trial.
4. All weapons surrendered during the amnesty period were supposed to be transported to the district headquarters for proper stocktaking by joint teams comprising district magistrates, police, and district administrations. Completion reports are still awaited.
5. No high-priority target raids have been conducted so far.
6. There is a marginal difference in routine recovery of weapons and recovery during the post-amnesty phase (165 weapons/day routinely; 400 weapons/day post-amnesty).
7. The confiscated weapons and ammunition were to be handed

over to the police and then systematically destroyed. So far only one such destruction has been reported, which brings up the question whether such confiscated weapons, if not properly stockpiled, are being mishandled and misused by law-enforcing agents themselves.

8. No efforts appear to have been made to curb the production/manufacture and pilferage of weapons from the principle source, viz., the tribal belts and the Darra arms bazaar.

DE-WEAPONIZATION IN BANGLADESH

The Bangladesh government launched two operations, Operation Clean Heart and Spider Web. Though the principal aim was to arrest the spiralling growth of terrorists, a related objective was to de-weaponize the society. Operation Clean Heart was launched in October 2002, and the government issued a directive on 5 November asking all licenced arms holders to deposit their weapons by 15 November: this deadline was later extended by a week due to poor response. The directive also banned trading in firearms of all types until further orders. Furthermore, security forces began raiding 'crime zones' in all parts of the country, including the capital, Dhaka. Only a small number of arms were deposited despite the government's warning that even legal weapons would be declared illegal if not deposited by the deadline.

The operation was called off in January 2003. During the drive, security forces seized 2,028 weapons and 29,754 rounds of ammunition. Considering that there are an estimated 200,000 illegal weapons in Bangladesh, with over 50,000 in Dhaka alone, Operation Clean Heart was not a success. This was because the government's efforts were politically targeted rather than being an anti-terrorism drive, resulting in human right's abuses.

Following Operation Clean Heart, in July 2003 the government launched another operation, Spider Web, targeting outlawed left-wing extremist parties active in the south-western districts of Kushtia, Chuadanga, Meherpur, Jessore, Khulna, Satkhira, and

Bagerhat. Even in this drive, the government failed to recover any significant numbers of weapons or ammunition.

TACKLING ILLEGAL PRODUCTION IN PAKISTAN

Bringing the Darra under the state umbrella is an issue that governments—past and present have seriously deliberated upon. As a necessary first step, the Tribal Areas were awarded the right to adult franchise, but the possibility of the manufacturers of Darra agreeing to any state supervision or taxation seems impossible, as was evident from the reaction faced by the government over its attempts to document and evaluate the economy.

At the practical level, this new de-weaponization policy will face many problems, especially in the NWFP and Tribal Areas where it is part of local culture and tradition to carry a weapon, and, in fact, forms part of their attire. This plan will definitely discourage open display of weapons in major urban centres, but again, this will not fully address the problem. Efforts made by past governments were inadequate, for they were either not properly formulated, or failed to curb the real root cause of the problem, which is the illicit trafficking of weapons. Whatever measures were enforced affected only the legal manufacturers, which gave the illegal trading cartels a free hand to conduct their business with impunity.

The flood of weaponry into the region has clearly played a major part in the erosion of law and order over the past decade. The growing proliferation of and access to small arms is increasing both the communal polarization and the incidence of violence. The very availability of weapons is providing a short-term solution for a long-term problem at the very point when political discourse and sound governance are required to overcome these problems, and the need is to harness efforts to combat this menace.

Providing the Darra gun manufacturers with alternate vocations at state-run factories has little monetary incentive for them. Convincing a sizeable population of the country, belonging mainly to the frontier or Tribal Areas, to give up their generations-old tradition of displaying guns is no easy task. State regulations may be effective in select urban belts where a sizeable number of the gun-carrying population is already licenced, but the main problem area is the unmarked, unlicenced, black-marketed weaponry which remains out of state control and very much in demand given the pervasive environment of conflict.

Darra is most infamous for manufacturing arms and ammunition. It has been in business. for almost a century. According to a survey conducted by the POF, there are about 60 small arms production units commonly referred to as 'factories'. In addition, there are about 300 small working places known as 'workshops', with four to five technicians working in each. There are about 400 shops of various sizes and capacities dealing in the sale of arms and ammunition. Although the exact number associated with the business is not known, it is generally claimed that at least 10,000 families are dependent on the arms industry. These include technicians, dealers and labourers. About 30 per cent of the workers belong to the settled areas, including 10 per cent from the Punjab province. In addition, a sizeable number of people are engaged in running small tea stalls, confectioneries and other provisions for the visiting public. Darra is a small area with a population of about 60,000, therefore, arms manufacturing and dealing is considered the lifeline of the area.

CHAPTER 6

Conclusion: The Way Forward

Faced with the lethal combination of technology and communications that give NSAs a distinct advantage, it is imperative that state parties think outside the traditional box of strategies and policies and evolve creative and innovative solutions to deep-rooted age-old problems like small arms.

Any attempt to resolve the issue of small arms needs to focus on arresting the supply as well as addressing the aspects related to demand. Focusing primarily on the supply might result in the evolution of two scenarios: first, the refining of illegal domestic production to cater to the increasing demand; and second, greater reliance on the use of IEDs. States need to be alert to both these scenarios while postulating appropriate mechanisms at national, regional, or international levels.

INTERNATIONAL MEASURES

At the international level, there has been some extent of cooperation on the POA. This cooperation can be positively utilized to *expand the POA* to include issues critical to the developing countries. The states could call for the following measures.

Expansion of the POA to Include a Comprehensive Debate on NSAs

The debate must not be restricted to the regulation/ban on the sale of weapons to NSAs, but should also include the postulation of possible future scenarios that might emerge should the POA be implemented successfully. The debate could also include exploring the linkages between the NSAs for the reasons explained earlier.

Expansion of the POA to Include a Comprehensive Debate on Explosives

An increased reliance on IEDs is the most likely fallout of a restricted supply of a small arms.

Expansion of the POA to Include a Comprehensive Debate on Illegal Production of Weapons

There is immediate need for a directive requesting member countries to monitor effective implementation of their various pieces of legislation pertaining to illegal manufacturing within their borders. According to the national report submitted as part of the POA, most countries do have appropriate legislations that ban illegal production. The problem lies not in lack of legislation, but in improper implementation.

More attention is also required to *monitor the interlinkages between the various NSAs*. This is particularly true of South Asia where the LTTE has taught the Naxalites the use of explosives, and an established linkage exists between the LTTE and the insurgents operating in India's north-east. Similarly, linkages between the Naxalite groups in India and the Maoists in Nepal cannot be disregarded. The debate on the network between various armed and criminal groups is imperative, because the linkages between them could be exploited to create a new supply network should the traditional supply network of arms be disturbed/dismantled by the increased national, regional, and international measures.

Of critical importance is also the need to *choke off the funds that provide militant groups with their purchasing power*. The ULFA spends more than 90 per cent of its monies from a thriving textile business in Bangladesh and extortion for purchasing arms. The financial and procurement network of the LTTE needs no elucidation. Unless the financial networks of the militant and criminal gangs are crippled through aggressive national and international measures, the problem will just appear in a different form in a different place.

The role played by the donor countries also needs to be explored. A cursory glace at security sector reforms underway in the Asia–Pacific point to the *pressure exerted by the donor countries* in ushering in a range of reforms. This leverage can also be utilized to create appropriate mechanisms and legislation relating to small arms in the recipient countries.

REGIONAL MEASURES

Despite discord amongst themselves, the South Asian countries can still cooperate against the proliferation of illicit weapons because it is entirely in their interest to do so. Pakistan is as vulnerable as India, and India as vulnerable as Bangladesh when it comes to the issue of small arms. There are no ambiguities about the danger these weapons can cause to the state and the society. Therefore, cooperation is a essential. As national implementation reports with regard to the POA reveal, all states are favourably disposed towards cooperating at the regional level. This enthusiasm could be tapped to arrive at a regional convention to arrest the flow of weapons into the region. When a SAARC convention on drugs exists, another on terrorism exists, why not a *SAARC convention on small arms*? A commitment to stall cross-border supply/movement of weapons might be ambitious given the political reality in South Asia. But a combined effort to keep weapons out of regional borders might not be difficult to obtain.

NATIONAL MEASURES

In countries like India, one of the reasons why people resort to the purchase of illegal weapons is because it is virtually impossible to obtain a legal one with the requisite licence. Relaxing licence restrictions would encourage people to procure legal weapons. This will also help the police to better track the illegal use of registered legal weapons. However, it must be pointed out that, though relaxed licensing might not result in the total conversion of the illegal sector into the legal sector, it might bring about a significant change in the overall law-and-order situation. Relaxed licensing norms could encourage a section of the illegal weapons clientele to go in for legal weapons. With a drop in demand, prices of these illegal weapons will go up. Once the price difference between legal and illegal weapons reduces, it is more than likely that even criminals might want to procure legal weapons rather than illegal ones. However, with regard to licensing, what suits India might not suit other states. Therefore, there is a need to *find the right balance between a relaxed and a rigid licensing regime.*

Individual states should engage in *better patrolling of their borders* by all agencies concerned with border management. This would help in keeping out not only small arms and light weapons, but also all illegal activity relating to narcotics and smuggling of contraband items.

The state is the only agency that can *target illegal domestic production.* Most states already have extensive legislation in place. What is required is its effective implementation. It is virtually impossible for any manufacturing unit to exist without the knowledge of the local police. Second, most illegally produced weapons rely on the availability of ammunition either in the black market or in the open market; the illegal manufacturing units produce only weapons and not ammunition. Here again, *stricter implementation of existing laws will suffice* to choke the easy availability of ammunition.

One suggestion that emerged from a study conducted on Small Arms and Human Insecurity under the aegis of the Small Arms Survey and the Colombo-based Regional Centre for Strategic Studies was the need for encouraging a community-based solution to the problem.[1] The suggestion, having emerged as a result of participatory rural appraisal, deserves serious thought. National governments need to sincerely invest in encouraging *a community-based solution* to the problem.

The drive to reduce the flow of small arms needs to be complemented with a drive to *address some of the critical issues that force people to take up arms.* These issues, resulting from entrenched

[1] Section iii, 'Community Responses', in *Small Arms and Human Insecurity, Reviewing Participatory Research in South Asia*, ed. Dipankar Banerji and Robert Muggah, Colombo: Regional Centre for Strategic Studies, and Small Arms Survey, July 2002, p. 41.

malgovernance, might well be within the realm of 'soft' security. But unless the states beset by perennial internal strife take measures that address some of these 'soft' security issues, there will be no 'state' left to face the 'hard' security issues when they emerge.

As mentioned earlier, the proliferation of small arms affects the state even when viewed within the narrow concept of State security, or studied through the comprehensive paradigm of human security. Therefore, it is imperative that states adopt the appropriate national, regional and international measures to ameliorate their situations and their society of the plague of small arms and light weapons. Despite all their efforts, states might not be able to fully rid their society of weapons. But that is not the aim either. The focus is more on *reducing* the use, and to that extent the states can be successful in bringing down the levels of violence.

RCSS PUBLICATIONS

- *Defence, Technology and Cooperative Security in South Asia: Report on the Proceedings of the Tenth Summer Workshop* (RCSS, 2004)
- *Environment Development and Human Security: Perspectives from South Asia* (2003)
- *Terrorism in South Asia: Impact on Development and Democratic Process* (SIPRA, 2003)
- *South Asia and the War on Terrorism* (India Research Press, 2003)
- *Shaping the Future–A South Asian Civil Society Dialogue* (RCSS, July 2002)
- *Small Arms and Human Insecurity* (RCSS, July 2002)
- *SAARC in the Twenty-First Century: Towards a Cooperative Future* (July 2002)
- *Memories of a Genocidal Partition: The Haunting Tale of Victims, Witnesses and Perpetrators* (RCSS, July 2002)
- *South Asian Security Futures: A Dialogue of Director's Regional Strategic Studies Institutes* (March 2002)
- *Security and Governance in South Asia* (September 2001)
- *Globalization and Non-Traditional Security in South Asia* (September 2001)
- *Security in the New Millennium* (India Research Press, 2001)
- *The Simla Agreement 1972: Its Wasted Promise* (Manohar, 2001)

RCSS Newsletter

A quarterly bulletin, it publishes a brief report of RCSS activities, presentations at its workshops on topics of contemporary interest and news and programmes of the RCSS and its alumnae.

RCSS Policy Studies

34 Indo-Pak Conflicts: Ripe to Resolve? (Manohar, 2005)
33 Small Arms and the Security Debate in South Asia (Manohar, 2005)
32 New Nuclear Triangle and China's Role in South Asia (forthcoming)
31 Stability through Economic Cooperation in a Nuclear Environment (Manohar, 2005)
30 Multi-Track Diplomacy between India and Pakistan: A Conceptual Framework for Sustainable Security (Manohar, 2005)
29 The Role of Mediation in Resolving India-Pakistan Conflict: Parameters and Possibilities (Manohar, 2005)
28 HIV/AIDS as a Security Threat to India (Manohar, 2005)
27 Nepal's Maoist Movement and Implications for India and China (Manohar, 2005)
26 Elite Perceptions in Foreign Policy: Role of Print Media in Influencing India-Pakistan Relations, 1989–1999 (Manohar, 2004)
25 Nuclar Risk Reduction Measures and Restraint Regime in South Asia (Manohar, 2004)
24 River Water Sharing Problem Between India and Pakistan: Case Study of the Indus Basin Water Treaty (June 2004)
23 Christianity and Political Conflict in India: The Case of Gujarat (June 2002)

Fellowship in South Asian Alternatives (FISAA) Monograph

- Water, Power And People: A South Asian Manifesto on the Politics and Knowledge of Water (1997)
- The Nuclear Debate: Ironies and Immoralities (1998)

Others

- *Directory of Individuals and Institutions Engaged in South Asian Strategic Studies* (1998).